TECHNOLOGY OF THE

F1

CAR

TECHNOLOGY OF THE

F1

CAR

Nigel Macknight

HAZLETON PUBLISHING

publisher
RICHARD POULTER

production manager
STEVEN PALMER

managing editor
PETER LOVERING

publishing development manager
SIMON MAURICE

business development manager
SIMON SANDERSON

sales promotion
CLARE KRISTENSEN

art editor
STEVE SMALL

photography by
BRYN WILLIAMS
with additional contributions by
LAT PHOTOGRAPHIC
ALLSPORT
TC ALLEN/PHOTOSPHERE
KEVIN CHEVIS
ILMOR ENGINEERING
CHRISTOPHER BENNETT

© Hazleton Publishing Limited, 1998

First published in 1998

ISBN 1-874557-87-X

Acknowledgements

For their co-operation in the research for this book, many thanks to: Steve Bryan of AP Racing; Tony Harrison and Barry Wainwright of Brookhouse Paxford; Elaine Catton Quinn, Nick Hayes and Denise Proctor of Cosworth Racing; Dick Jones of Cranfield Impact Centre; Alistair Watkins of the FIA; Dermot Bambridge and Carol Dawes of Goodyear Racing; David Williams of Speedline Sport; and Cliff Hawkins and Derrick Worthington of Xtrac.

Printed in Hong Kong through World Print

distributors

UNITED KINGDOM	NORTH AMERICA	AUSTRALIA	NEW ZEALAND	SOUTH AFRICA
Biblios Ltd	Motorbooks International	Technical Book and Magazine	David Bateman Ltd	Motorbooks
Star Road	PO Box 1, 729 Prospect Ave.	Co. Pty	PO Box 100-242	341 Jan Smuts Avenue
Partridge Green	Osceola	295 Swanston Street	North Shore Mail Centre	Craighall Park
West Sussex RH13 8LD	Wisconsin 54020, USA	Melbourne, Victoria 3000	Auckland 1330	Johannesburg
Tel: 01403 710971	Tel: (1) 715 294 3345	Tel: (03) 9663 3951	Tel: (9) 415 7664	Tel: (011) 325 4458/60
Fax: 01403 711143	Fax: (1) 715 294 4448	Fax: (03) 9663 2094	Fax: (9) 415 8892	Fax: (011) 325 4146

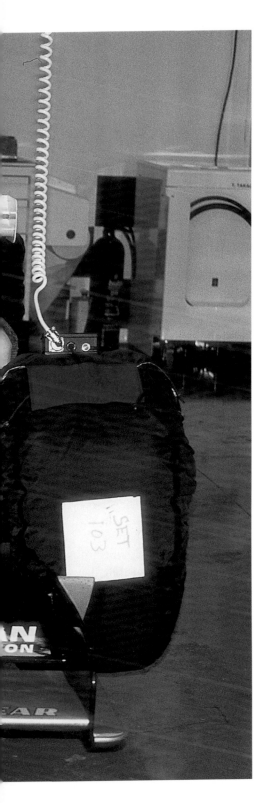

CONTENTS

introduction

DEFINING THE CONCEPT

THE governing body for Formula 1 is the Fédération Internationale de l'Automobile (FIA), headquartered in Paris under the presidency of Max Mosley. Central to the technical regulations it promulgates for the Formula 1 World Championship is the requirement that teams must design and manufacture their own cars. They cannot purchase a proprietary chassis in the way that, for example, most of the teams in the CART Championship do.

This book is intended to illuminate the process by which Formula 1 teams create their cars – placing particular emphasis on racetrack action to illustrate the key principles.

FIA technical regulations dictate the form the cars will take to such an extent that they all look very similar. There are regulations governing the overall length of the cars, their width, their height, the dimensions of their aerodynamic appendages and the amount by which they overhang the front and rear wheels – and a great many other dimensional limitations – all policed by mounting templates in strategic positions on the car and taking measurements from them. There are also restrictions on the degree to which innovative technological solutions can be applied to the eternal conundrum of 'going faster'.

This is somewhat unfortunate, because spectators are denied the opportunity to see radically different designs which reflect a fresh perspective on how performance might be enhanced. Bold leaps in design philosophy – spectacularly demonstrated by the six-wheel Tyrrells of 1976-77 and the infamous Brabham 'fan car' of 1978 – have given way to a more circumspect, less visible, approach to innovation.

In days past, the skills of an exceptional driver could make up for the deficiencies of an improperly designed car, but that is no longer the case. The plain fact is, in Formula 1 today, the chief car designer is as valuable to a team as its number one driver – and, as a consequence, designers have become increasingly well paid. When former Williams designer Adrian Newey joined the McLaren team in August 1997, he did so for a reputed salary of £2 million and a seven-figure signing fee.

It is no coincidence that Newey, pictured here, initially trained as an aerodynamicist, for aerodynamics has become the single most important facet of Formula 1 car design.

In sharp contrast to earlier eras, when individual designers were credited with designing entire cars almost single-handedly, today's cars are designed by a large *team* of designers, due to the sheer complexity of the task. Nevertheless, there is usually one individual with over-riding governance of the essential concept who leads the others: for example, Ross Brawn at Ferrari, Pat Symonds at Benetton and Alan Jenkins at Stewart. Others then play vital roles undertaking specific aspects of the design: aerodynamicists, composites engineers, transmission designers and so forth.

The top teams employ 30–35 design personnel – many of whom are 'detail draughtsmen' assisting the key individuals by fleshing out specific aspects of the design – and, typically, employ a further 20 in research and development.

The regulations effectively define the order in which the key elements of Formula 1 cars are laid out, front to back. Starting at the front, the driver's feet must be a mandatory minimum distance behind the front axle line, for safety reasons. Working back from that, the fuel load must be stored entirely behind the driver, again for safety reasons. The engine and gearbox will inevitably be located behind the fuel load, so there is little or no scope for an innovative chassis layout.

Even if the regulations were freer, the dimensions of some elements of the car cannot be significantly altered by any designer – most notably the dimensions of the cockpit, which must be generous enough to accommodate the driver in relative comfort and safety. Although car designers have some influence over engine design, there is a physical limit to how compact an engine of a given capacity can be. A gearbox, too – with all of its ratios to accommodate – can only be so small.

The process of designing a new car tends to be evolutionary rather than revolutionary. There is a strong tendency to make an existing concept better, rather than discard it totally and start over. In fact, a certain percentage of components are actually carried over from the previous year's car in the interests of reliability – particularly those components which have no direct impact on lap times: for example, components within the fuel system.

There are typically four phases in the design of a Formula 1 car: conceptual scheming, preliminary scheming, final scheming and detailing. Design activities are very much computer-based, with a wide range of software being employed throughout the process. The majority of teams have made a total transition away from paper engineering drawings in favour of Computer-Aided Design (CAD) – so draughtsmanship has been supplanted by 'CAD modelling', in which shapes are generated entirely digitally and represented on-screen in either two-dimensional or quasi-3D form.

Formidable computer power then allows designers to manipulate the models at will. They can alter them when design changes are necessary, and can 'rotate' components to view them from an almost infinite number of perspectives, and in cross-section at any point (station) along their length.

Once the designer has input a design change, all of the necessary calculations and draughtsmanship are undertaken by the computer software, which presents the end result almost instantaneously – avoiding the time-consuming task of creating new sets of conventional paper drawings every time something is changed.

Rather than purchasing the necessary hardware and software, most of which is extremely expensive, many teams enter into commercial arrangements with manufacturers – such as Hewlett Packard (Jordan) and Parametrics (Tyrrell) – whereby it is provided free of charge as a form of sponsorship.

When a CAD system is linked to a group of machine tools, the capability is extended to become Computer-Aided Manufacture (CAM), allowing components which have been modelled on-screen to be partially or wholly manufactured virtually independent of human intervention, saving precious time.

FIA regulations stipulate that the *combined* weight of the car, driver and on-board fluids must at no time fall below 600 kg (1323 lb). To verify that cars meet this requirement, FIA inspectors frequently position them on four hyper-sensitive pressure pads, then ask the driver to stand on one pad for the combined weight to be measured with great accuracy.

Designers make strenuous efforts to prevent their cars being overweight – mindful of the fact that every kilogram over the minimum permissible weight adds about 0.03 second to each lap: 5 kg (11 lb) of excess weight would therefore translate into a 12-second deficit over a typical race distance. Most teams manage to build their cars *below* the minimum weight limit (even the weight of the paint is kept to a minimum), then add blocks of lead ballast to bring them back up to the required minimum – positioning the ballast so as to assist in achieving the desired weight distribution. The lead is placed low down, to help keep the car's centre of gravity as low as possible.

Achieving a low centre of gravity is a key objective in the design process, because it makes the car more stable under heavy cornering, braking and acceleration forces. The weight distribution is also critically important, because distributing the weight more evenly between the front and rear of the car allows both sets of tyres to contribute more effectively to the overall performance and handling. Designers attempt to bring weight forward as much as possible, because the car's heaviest components – the engine, the gearbox and the fuel load – are unavoidably concentrated at the rear, placing a proportionately greater burden on the rear tyres.

Above all other factors, the key to designing a successful Formula 1 car is achieving an excellent aerodynamic performance. Aerodynamic devices abound on the modern Formula 1 car. The most visible are the complex arrays of aerofoil surfaces mounted at the front and rear of the cars, which generate huge downforce and thus provide greater levels of grip in the corners. But there are other aerodynamic devices almost hidden from view – such as the undertray, which works in conjunction with an upward-sloping 'ramp' at the rear of the car (the rear diffuser) to generate even more downforce and grip.

Mechanical – as opposed to aerodynamic – grip is another vitally important quality. This derives from the car's weight distribution and suspension geometry, and the performance of the differential and the tyres.

Blending the aerodynamic and mechanical qualities into a winning package is the goal of all Formula 1 car designers.

A major change in the technical regulations was introduced prior to the 1998 season. The cars had to be 20 cm (7.88 in) – ten per cent – narrower than before, and had now to be fitted with grooved tyres.

The effects of these and other new regulations on the performance of Formula 1 cars have been manifold, and are among the subjects explored in the following chapters.

chapter 1 THE CHASSIS

A FORMULA 1 chassis is structurally very complex, because the forces acting upon it are themselves extremely complex. This is not surprising, as it is the central structural element of the car, with virtually all of the other load-bearing elements attached directly to it. There are powerful and wildly fluctuating forces being fed in through the front suspension as it responds to high cornering and braking forces, and absorbs bumps in the racetrack surface. There are massive bending loads being fed in at the engine mounts, and brutal twisting forces, too, because this is the structural joint where the front half of the car – the chassis – is attached to the rear half: the engine, gearbox, rear suspension and rear aerofoil assemblies, all fixed together to form a single structure.

Additional twisting forces are fed in at the engine mounts by the torque effect from the engine when the driver accelerates hard.

At the opposite end of the chassis, huge aerodynamic loads are fed in via the nosebox from the downforce generated by the front aerofoil assemblies. Substantial forces are also imposed from beneath the chassis – from downforce generated by the undertray – and from its flanks, from the interplay between the sidepods and the airflow rushing over and through them.

The chassis even has loads imposed on it from within, because the G-forces from the driver's body are fed in from his seat and safety harness attachments.

Because it generally takes the longest time to produce, the chassis is usually the first element of the car to have its design committed to the manufacturing process. Although almost all of the Formula 1 teams produce their chassis in-house, at least one front-running team subcontracts the task to a specialist manufacturer.

Formula 1 chassis are produced almost entirely from carbon-composite materials: in the case of the chassis, the term 'composite' means a combination of two skins of multi-ply carbonfibre sandwiching a layer of aluminium honeycomb material. However, the term can also be applied to the carbonfibre itself, as it is a composite of the carbon fibres and a pre-impregnated epoxy resin. Pre-impregnating the fibres ensures that the resin is evenly distributed, guaranteeing consistency in the make-up and performance of the finished product once the resin has been hardened (cured) by the application of extreme heat and pressure.

To simplify production, the chassis is built in several pieces – known as panels – then bonded together. The largest panel constitutes virtually the entire chassis, and is a complex one-piece structure which only a few years ago would have been made in three pieces: the upper and lower chassis halves, plus a separate rollover hoop. Smaller panels include the chassis floor, two internal bulkheads – known as the seat-back and the dash bulkhead – and the (removable) nosebox.

Before the panels themselves can be produced, a full-sized pattern must be built for each panel. From these, moulds are made, then the carbon-composite materials are laid up in the moulds to make the panels themselves.

To deal with such complex forces effectively, and contribute to the overall performance and handling of the car, a fundamental design objective is to create sufficient stiffness to prevent the chassis flexing. Here, the requirement is for both torsional stiffness (a resistance to twisting loads) and beam stiffness (a resistance to either lateral or longitudinal bending loads). Another fundamental design objective is to create sufficient impact resistance: the chassis should be resilient enough to protect its driver in the event of an accident, and must be proved to be so to the FIA's satisfaction in a rigorous series of crash tests.

There is a potential conflict between the need for stiffness and the need for impact resistance – because with any carbonfibre material, the more stiffness it offers, the less resilience it has. Designers resolve this conflict by conceiving a smoothly flowing shape which spreads impact loads evenly, rather than introducing sharp corners which concentrate them. Here, again, there is a potential conflict – because aerodynamic considerations play a key role in determining the shape of the chassis, so a design compromise must be reached.

The Williams team, based at Grove, is among the few in Formula 1 to have truly perfected chassis design. Following the departure of Adrian Newey to McLaren, Williams's chief designer is Gavin Fisher, working under technical director Patrick Head.

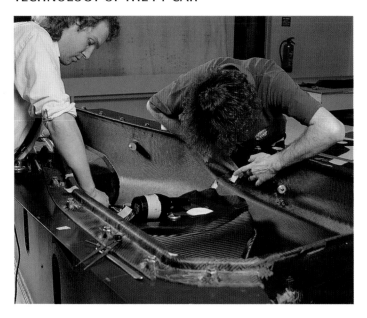

The chassis's inner and outer carbonfibre skins are each typically composed of between five and seven layers of varying material thicknesses and types, but in regions where greater strength and/or rigidity are required there might be as many as several dozen layers.

By laying up the individual pieces of carbonfibre so that their fibres are oriented in particular directions, it is possible to transfer incoming loads to specific places within the structure, or to dissipate them over a wider area. For example, it may be desirable to distribute an incoming load to a part of the chassis where reinforcements lie, in which case multiple layers will be oriented so that their fibres run in that direction. Conversely, if multiple layers are oriented so that the fibres run in a *variety* of directions, loads will be dissipated over a wide area. The types of carbonfibre specified for each region, layer on layer, vary according to the nature of the loads which must be dealt with there.

Given the complexity of both the chassis structure and the forces acting upon it, calculating the most effective way to build a strong, rigid, resilient, lightweight structure would be nightmarishly difficult, were it not for advanced computing power.

Of the many advanced computer-based techniques applied in the design and manufacture of Formula 1 cars, the key technique employed to determine the physical make-up of the chassis is Finite Element Analysis (FEA).

Like carbonfibre, FEA found its way into race-car design from the aerospace industry. It is a computerised method of predicting and analysing the structural characteristics of key components at the design stage with a high degree of accuracy, and Formula 1 designers employ it to help create components which are structurally highly efficient, yet also very lightweight. Although the structural characteristics of a component such as a chassis are infinitely complex, by breaking the structure down into a finite number of elements by computer, it becomes possible to analyse its behaviour under the influence of a wide variety of loads and calculate the most effective way to manufacture it.

Whilst analysing the structural characteristics of the chassis under particular loads, the composites engineer assesses the effect of adding a further layer of carbonfibre to a particular region in a particular orientation, then taking it away again – thereby quantifying its contribution to the overall structural performance. Generally speaking, his aim is to achieve his structural objectives with the minimum amount of material, thereby saving weight.

It is a tribute to the skill of composites engineers that a bare Formula 1 chassis typically weighs just 35 kg (80 lb), yet is capable of transferring around 750 hp to the racetrack and withstanding at least two tons of aerodynamic downforce.

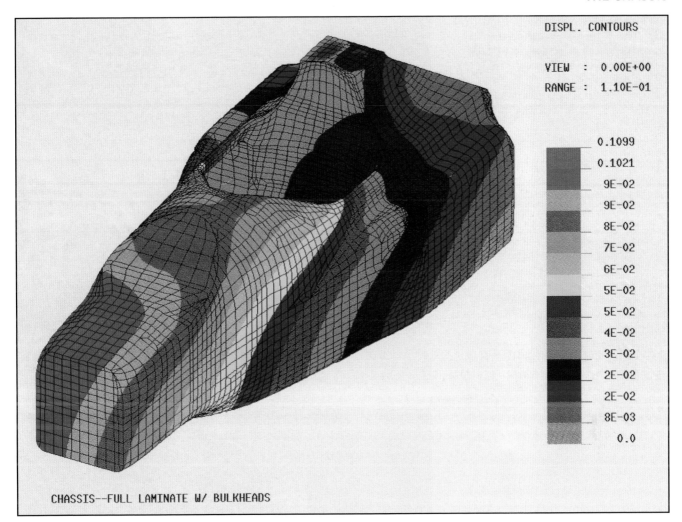

DISPL. CONTOURS

VIEW : 0.00E+00

RANGE : 1.10E-01

	0.1099
	0.1021
	9E-02
	9E-02
	8E-02
	7E-02
	6E-02
	5E-02
	5E-02
	4E-02
	3E-02
	2E-02
	2E-02
	8E-03
	0.0

CHASSIS--FULL LAMINATE W/ BULKHEADS

Formula 1 teams have specialist composites engineers within their design groups to conduct FEA. Once an analysis is completed, the results are displayed to them in graphical form, with values colour-coded to aid interpretation. This is a major advance on early FEA systems, which presented data in a user *un*friendly raw numerical form. In addition, the deformations (flexing) of a component can be represented in such a way that extremely small movements are artifically exaggerated, making it easier to identify the areas where movement is taking place.

Without FEA, a greater margin for error would have to be factored into the chassis construction, and the resulting structure would be heavier than necessary, rendering the car uncompetitive. Worse still, if the margin was insufficient, structural breakages would occur and the car would be downright dangerous. Identifying stress concentrations likely to result in structural failure - allowing designers to eliminate them - is a key FEA capability.

TECHNOLOGY OF THE F1 CAR

The first step in actually manufacturing the chassis panels is producing the patterns. This stage in the gestation of a car marks the transition from CAD (Computer-Aided Design) to CAM (Computer-Aided Manufacture), because the same computer software used to design the car now helps with the process of physically building it.

Although there are several different techniques for producing Formula 1 chassis panel patterns, and teams have their own preferred methods, they all produce essentially the same results. The method described here is the most common, and begins when the appropriate data from the CAD system are fed into an automated routing machine, which fashions the patterns from either a proprietary pattern-making material – usually Ureol – or from mahogany, the preference of a few teams.

Ureol is a Ciba-Giegy product which is delivered in slab form. Although it is a man-made material, it has many similar properties to wood. However, it is easier to work, being grainless, and is virtually impervious to moisture-retention and thermal expansion, so patterns made from Ureol retain their size and shape very precisely. As supplied, slabs of Ureol are only 5 cm (2 in) thick, so the larger patterns must be made by stacking and gluing several slabs together beforehand.

The pattern-making material is secured firmly to a surface table beneath the router head to prevent any slippage while cutting takes place. The router head moves in swathes, back and forth, removing material with relentless precision until the required form is created.

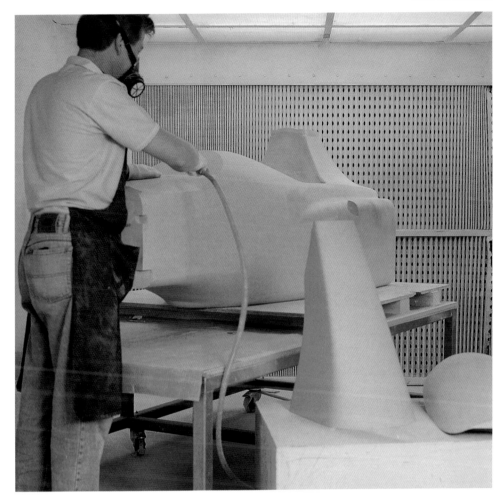

When all of the patterns constituting the chassis have been produced in this way, they are bolted together temporarily so that their external surfaces can be sanded by hand with wet-or-dry paper. This process is called 'shaping through', and it ensures that the interfaces between adjoining patterns blend smoothly from one to the other. It also removes the faint machining marks left by the router - otherwise they would subsequently become imprinted on the moulds, and thus be transferred to the external surfaces of the completed chassis.

A coat of epoxy paint is then applied to each of the chassis patterns to protect them from chemical attack by the resins in the carbonfibre when the moulds are laid up on them at the next stage of the process. The patterns are then ovened at a specified temperature to harden the paint - and stabilise it by releasing any volatile chemicals - then they are hand-sanded with very fine wet-or-dry paper and rubbed with T-Cut to produce a smooth surface finish.

Finally, the chassis patterns are temporarily bolted back together and fixed to a large surface table, so that a three-axis digitising machine can 'scan' the full pattern and confirm that its shape is faithful to the original CAD data.

The moulds from which the carbon-composite chassis panels will be produced are made by laying up carbon-fibre on the patterns to form a 'reflected' reproduction of the end product. Carbonfibre is used for the moulds because it offers good resistance to the expansion and distortion which would otherwise occur when the moulds are exposed to the very high temperatures necessary to cure the chassis panels.

Before mould-making can get under way, the patterns must be thoroughly prepared. A ledge - known as a weir or return - is added to the outer perimeter of each pattern, so that the finished moulds will have a strengthening, stiffening angle around their edges when they are removed from their patterns. Some of the moulds will be made in several pieces to aid removal of the completed panels - particularly in cases where a panel might otherwise become 'trapped' in its mould - so additional weirs are incorporated at the divisions.

To ensure that the finished moulds will separate cleanly, each pattern is given several coats of a release agent and buffed to a high sheen with several coats of hard wax.

Only then does mould-making begin: the procedures are similar to those employed when the chassis panels themselves are produced - described next - except that the moulds have very modest structural requirements, and therefore have only a single-skin construction with no aluminium honeycomb sandwich layer.

This photograph shows a mould for the lower half of a chassis, but this 'top and bottom' method has now been supplanted.

Before laying-up of the chassis panels can take place, the moulds must be thoroughly prepared. Each mould is degreased (usually with a solvent such as Acetone) to remove any contaminants, then receives as many as ten coats of a release agent. Each coat is left to evaporate before the next application, and the surface is buffed to maintain a high surface sheen. The mould is then ovened to harden the release agent, baking it into the surface.

This lengthy procedure only applies to the first use of each mould. For the production of subsequent panels, the moulds are given just a single coat of release agent.

Finally, a series of small, removable patterns known as tooling blocks are fitted into the mould. By laying up carbonfibre around the tooling blocks, apertures and recesses can be formed in panels: for example, at the points where the foremost wishbone mounts will be recessed into the chassis, and where the aft legs of the front wishbones will pass through apertures in the chassis sides. Apertures and recesses like these are usually incorporated to improve the streamlining at points where wishbone mounts and other such protuberances would induce aerodynamic drag.

Other, much smaller, tooling blocks are fitted at points where narrow passages are required for electrical cabling, hydraulic-fluid pipes and suchlike to pass through the finished panels.

The positions of the tooling blocks were plotted earlier, on the patterns – by the three-axis digitising machine, drawing upon CAD data – and were 'reflected' in the moulds in the form of holes drilled in precisely the required positions and tapped to accept them.

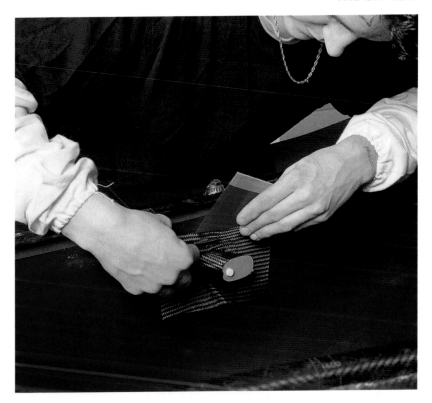

The laying-up of carbon-composite materials within the moulds to form the chassis panels is a meticulous process, in which highly skilled laminators closely follow explicit written and diagrammatical instructions prescribed by the composites engineer as a result of his earlier work on the computer, conducting FEA. Indeed, the composites engineer stands in close attendance when the first example of each panel is being laid up, adjusting the precise manner in which the materials are assembled in the mould in a way that is only possible now that the job has departed the theoretical world of computational predictions and can at last be viewed in true 3D.

While the process of producing the inner and outer carbonfibre skins of the chassis panels is essentially the same as that employed for the production of the moulds, the laying-up of the carbonfibre pieces in this case involves far more complex combinations of material-types and fibre-orientations – all painstakingly tailored to create the specific high-performance structural properties of each particular panel.

It is essential, when laying up the carbonfibre, that the material conforms to the contours of the mould and does not bridge any of the corners or other features, so the laminators warm it through with hair-dryers to soften the resin, making the fabric more pliable. The fact that the resin is already within the fibres simplifies the task of laying up the carbonfibre, as it makes the material slightly sticky at room temperature, preventing it from slipping from vertical surfaces after it has been pressed on. This quality is known as 'tack'.

In addition to hair-dryers, the laminators use surgical blades and spatulas to work the material into and around the features of the mould, and around the tooling blocks, taking care to ensure that pockets of air do not become trapped between plies. Adjoining pieces of carbonfibre are overlapped to create a thoroughly integrated structure. The carbonfibre pieces, as supplied to them, are slightly oversized so that the laminators can trim them down to create precisely the correct amount of overlap.

After the first two or three layers have been laid up, steps are taken to compact them together and force them against the contours of the mould to ensure a faithful reproduction of the intended form. This is achieved by enveloping the mould/panel combination in a carefully tailored vacuum bag and placing it in a large pressurised chamber known as an autoclave, where it is subjected to a combination of a high vacuum state and a moderate temperature rise. This process is known as 'consolidation and debulking', and it is repeated several times as the layers of carbonfibre are built up.

As part of this process, there are various options for simultaneously drawing off the excess resin which 'bleeds out' of the carbonfibre. The precise amount of resin drawn off depends upon the fibre-to-resin ratio the composites engineer wishes to achieve: this has a critical bearing on the structural performance of the end product. A layer of cotton wool-like polyester cloth known as a breather layer is sandwiched between the outer layer of carbonfibre and the inner face of the vacuum bag, upon which excess resin and various volatile chemicals become deposited. A non-stick film known as a release layer, placed between the breather layer and the carbonfibre, ensures that the two do not stick together.

Yet another layer – this time a rigid (aluminium or carbon-composite) layer known variously as a pressure plate, a caul plate, or an intensifier – can also be employed, again optionally, to bring more direct pressure down onto the carbonfibre layers.

When all of the carbonfibre layers which constitute a complete skin have been laid up in the mould, the mould/panel combination is enveloped in a vacuum bag once again and returned to the autoclave. This time, the vacuum state within the bag is augmented by much higher temperatures, and also by extreme pressure (as high as 100 psi) – compressing the layers tight together to produce a super-strong structure.

A complete skin is usually subjected to these conditions for around two and a half hours, which cures it – turning it rock hard. The skin is only a few millimetres thick when completed.

Chassis panels are autoclaved three times during the manufacturing process: once after the first carbonfibre skin has been laid up, again after the aluminium honeycomb sandwich layer has been incorporated, and a third and final time after the second skin has been laid up.

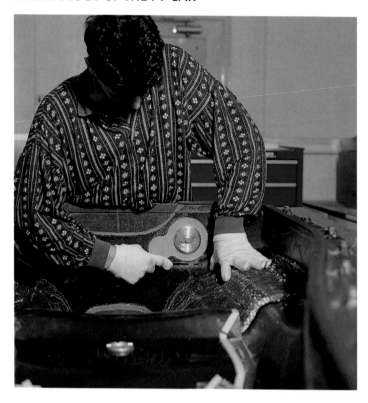

The layer of aluminium honeycomb material sandwiched between the two carbonfibre skins varies significantly in thickness, depending upon the predicted structural demands on that particular region of the chassis, as calculated by the composites engineer at the FEA stage. The honeycomb is supplied to the laminators in pre-cut form and must be positioned with great precision, because if it does not adhere evenly to both skins, the structural loads will be unevenly distributed.

A sheet of neat resin is applied between the skins and the aluminium honeycomb sandwich layer, creating an exceptionally strong bond when cured.

At points where bolts and other types of fasteners will pass through the structure to retain suspension components, and fittings such as the driver's safety harness anchors will be attached, localised reinforcements known as inserts are set into the aluminium honeycomb material. Without them, the bolts would move about under the forces acting upon them, crushing the honeycomb material and fracturing the carbonfibre skins. The inserts are supplied to the laminator in pre-cut form, each with a hole drilled through the middle, and are typically made from either solid aluminium or a very high-density resin-impregnated fabric material tradenamed Tufnol.

As with the tooling blocks, the location of each insert is preordained – having been determined by the composites engineer at the FEA stage, plotted on the patterns by the three-axis digitising machine, and 'reflected' in the moulds in the form of PTFE dowels protruding from holes drilled in precisely the required positions to accept them (the dowels will simply break when the panel is eventually prised from its mould).

After another spell in the autoclave, the second skin is laid up, then any tooling blocks fitted to that particular mould are removed to allow the panel to be prised away and sent for 'finishing' and integration into a complete chassis structure.

Two chassis panels have to be removable: the nosebox and the damper cover (the latter is situated immediately in front of the cockpit aperture and covers the inboard elements of the front suspension system). The nosebox is produced in exactly the same manner as the other chassis panels, with two skins of carbonfibre sandwiching a layer of aluminium honeycomb material. The damper cover is produced in a slightly different way: because it is not a load-bearing component, it has a single-skin construction with no honeycomb layer.

The quantity of chassis panels produced varies according to the anticipated attrition rate for each panel type. Needless to say, noseboxes tend to be produced in the largest quantities!

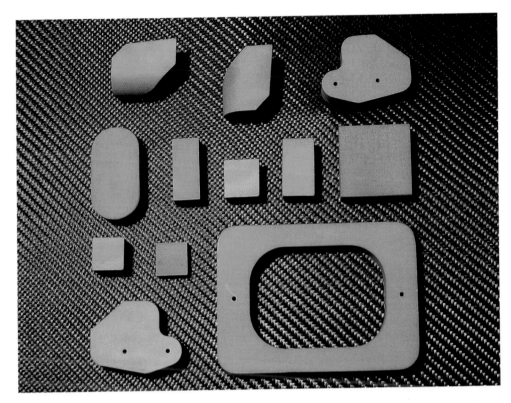

Before the main chassis panel is permanently 'closed' by the bonding-on of the floor panel, the two internal bulkheads are bonded in with epoxy adhesive. One is the seat-back (pictured here): a sculpted carbon-composite/aluminium honeycomb sandwich panel located directly behind the driver's seat, forming a partition between the fuel cell compartment and the cockpit. The other is the dash bulkhead: a flat 'hoop' through which the driver's legs pass, made in the same way as the seat-back and located just forward of the cockpit aperture.

These bulkheads contribute to the overall strength and rigidity of the chassis by providing internal reinforcement and countering any tendency it might have to lozenge under cornering or impact loads.

'Finishing' of chassis panels primarily involves enlarging, and/or tapping and/or countersinking the holes in the various inserts where all of the internal and external components will be mounted later (access to awkward areas is easier while the chassis is still in pieces). Some teams have sophisticated five-axis automated drilling machines to undertake this task, but many prefer to do it manually using a system of templates. Either way, the chassis panels are anchored squarely to steel jigs to ensure a high standard of accuracy.

Typical examples of the locations of these holes are: on the top of the main chassis panel, at the points where the inboard elements of the front suspension will be mounted; at the front of that panel, for the nosebox attachments and the front wishbone mountings; on the sides of that panel, for the sidepod attachments; at the rear of that panel, for the engine mounts; and on the floor panel, where the aerodynamic undertray will be mounted.

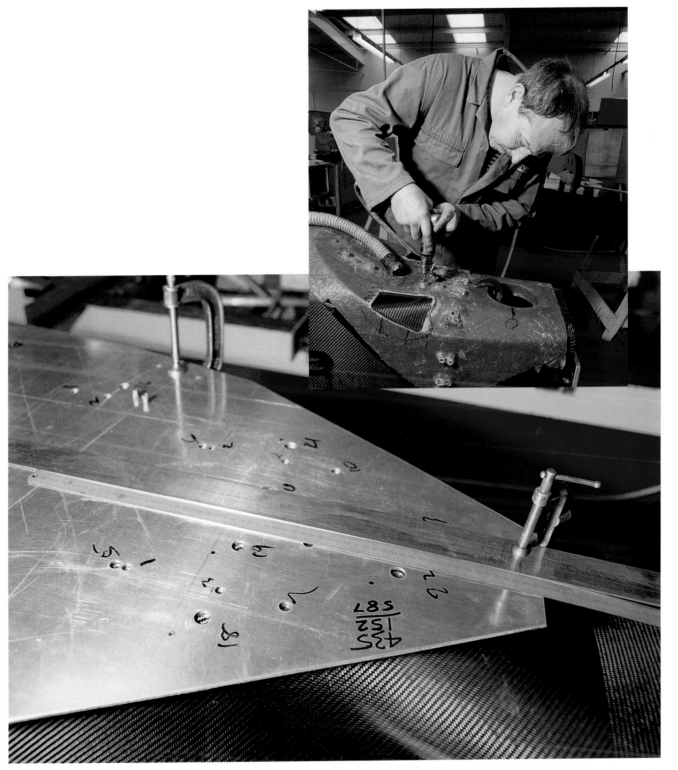

chapter 2 CRASH-TESTING

TO ENSURE that drivers are properly protected in the event of an accident, the FIA insists that teams put their new cars through a rigorous crash-testing programme. The accidents which claimed the lives of Roland Ratzenberger and Ayrton Senna during the tragic 1994 San Marino Grand Prix meeting accelerated the introduction of a sweeping series of safety improvements. Other deeply unsettling accidents subsequently provided further impetus – perhaps most notably Karl Wendlinger's near-fatal crash during practice for the 1994 Monaco Grand Prix, which highlighted the need for greater head protection.

From the start of the 1997 season, it has been mandatory for Formula 1 cars to carry an aircraft-style 'black box' to record vital information which would help investigators to identify the cause of a serious accident. The delay in identifying the reasons for Ayrton Senna's fatal crash prompted the decision to introduce these devices. Drivers', and indeed spectators', safety is taken increasingly seriously – and rightly so. At the 1997 British Grand Prix, for example, there were 50 doctors on duty around the racetrack and in the circuit medical centre – including many specialists in fields such as neurology and burn injuries – supported by 25 ambulances and their crews.

Seven out of the eleven Formula 1 teams have their crash-testing undertaken at the Cranfield Impact Centre (CIC), part of the Cranfield Institute of Technology near Bedford, England, which they hire for around £2500 a day: they are the British-based Williams, Benetton, Tyrrell, Jordan, Stewart and Arrows teams, and the French-based Prost equipe. McLaren is unique among the British-based teams in not using CIC for crash-testing: it tests at the Motor Industry Research Association (MIRA) facility in Nuneaton, not far from Cranfield. The two Italian-based teams – Ferrari and Minardi – go to a test facility in their home country; the Swiss-based Sauber team tests at the same place.

The crash-test photos in this chapter were taken at CIC in Cranfield, but all of these test sites have broadly similar facilities.

The FIA-regulated Formula 1 crash-test programme is designed to simulate a wide spectrum of impact scenarios. The first and most spectacular crash test simulates a head-on collision, and is designed to assess two things: the ability of the nosebox to protect the driver's feet and ankles from serious injury; and the ability of the chassis structure in general, and the nosebox in particular, to dissipate the kinetic energy which is released at the moment of impact, so that the driver is saved from injurious deceleration forces.

When the 'frontal impact test' is undertaken at Cranfield Impact Centre, the test criteria are met by propelling the chassis with a system of bungee cords down a 15-metre (50-ft) ramp inclined at an angle of 11 degrees, to impact a steel plate 25 mm (1 in) thick. The steel plate is immovable, being set in a huge concrete block.

FIA regulations for the frontal impact test stipulate a minimum impact speed of 12 metres per second (39.4 feet per second) – a little under 45 kph (30 mph). Such a speed may seem unrepresentative of an actual Formula 1 collision, but bear in mind that by the time a chassis strikes anything of substance, much of its energy will already have been dissipated by friction in a gravel run-off area and the deformation of the suspension – and that a length of guardrail protected by layers of tyres yields considerably.

The FIA-regulation steel plate used in the crash test, on the other hand, yields *not an inch*!

When the steel plate is struck, average deceleration of the chassis must not exceed 25 G. Peak deceleration values are considerably higher, but only momentary. Damage must be limited to the nosebox itself: it must not extend beyond the interface with the chassis.

To assess the effect on the car's occupant, and thereby verify the ability of the chassis and nosebox to dissipate frontal impact forces, a 75 kg (165 lb) anthropomorphic mannequin rides in the cockpit, firmly strapped in by a multi-point safety harness of the type approved for Grand Prix racing. An accelerometer is installed in the chest of the mannequin to measure the deceleration forces at the moment of impact. FIA regulations stipulate that these forces must not exceed 60 G for more than three milliseconds.

In order to increase the correlation of the frontal impact test to a real accident, the chassis is fitted with a fuel cell – filled with water – and a loaded cockpit fire extinguisher, reproducing the structural loadings these items would generate in a race-track impact. The chassis is attached at the engine mounting points to a sturdy tubular-steel sled which serves as 'transport' for the rapid trip down the ramp, and also replicates the mass of the car aft of the chassis – namely, the cumulative mass of the engine, gearbox, drivetrain, rear suspension assemblies, brakes, uprights, wheels, and rear aerofoil assemblies. CIC's sled weighs 430 kg (946 lb).

FIA regulations demand that the minimum weight of the entire chassis/sled combination must be 780 kg (1716 lb) – to simulate conditions in an actual race – so lead ballast may have to be added.

TECHNOLOGY OF THE F1 CAR

An electric hoist drives a length of chain which hauls the chassis/sled combination backwards up the ramp. It is held by steel jaws for a short time at a predetermined point near the top while final instrumentation checks are completed and all but one operative evacuates to the safety of a bunker. The lone operative then removes a safety bolt and retires to a respectful distance.

When the steel jaws are released, the chassis literally *flies* down the ramp, because its supporting sled is borne on four air-bearings instead of wheels. Although there *are* four small rollers on the side of the sled which momentarily glance rails on the edges of the ramp on the way down – guiding it straight and true – the run is virtually frictionless, ensuring consistency from run to run.

At the point of impact, a report akin to a rifle shot resounds around the walls of the test building. If all has gone according to plan, the nosebox should have collapsed progressively, absorbing the energy of the impact, but there should be no other damage. The FIA inspector pays particular attention to the condition of the mountings for the driver's safety harness and the cockpit fire extinguisher.

Two accelerometers mounted on the sled measure its deceleration. Data from either is sufficient to support the test, for each acts as a backup to the other should one fail at the moment of impact. The precise impact speed is measured by photo-electric cells.

A single videotape of the whole event is recorded by a high-speed camera running at, typically, 2000 frames per second. A confidentiality agreement between the team and the test centre ensures that the technologically sensitive footage does not fall into the hands of rival teams.

It surprises many people to learn that the chassis which undergoes the frontal impact test, the so-called 'datum chassis', not only must undergo all of the other crash-tests, but also usually goes on to actually *race* – following repairs where necessary – as do subsequent chassis put through some of the other crash-tests. Subsequent chassis must weigh within five per cent of the weight of the datum chassis, and must be proved to be structurally identical.

When a chassis has passed all of the required tests, the FIA inspector signifies its crashworthiness by applying a special plate, sealed on with tamper-proof paint.

Since the start of the 1997 season, Formula 1 cars have had to be fitted with a rear-impact absorption structure to protect the driver if he is 'assaulted' from behind by another car, or spins off backwards and strikes something solid. The rear-impact absorption structure is fitted onto the back of the gearbox and is of essentially the same carbon-composite construction as the nosebox, but is smaller and its shape varies more from one car type to another. Its effectiveness is verified by a 'rear impact test'.

The same ramp and sled employed for the frontal impact test are used for the rear impact test – but in this case, instead of the relevant part of the car moving, it stays at the foot of the ramp and is struck by the sled. More specifically, the *gearbox* of the car under test, with its rear-impact absorption structure fitted – but no rear suspension or rear aerofoil elements – is firmly bolted to the fixed steel plate at the bottom of the ramp, mounted at the points where it would normally be bolted to the engine. A steel plate measuring 45 x 55 cm (17.72 x 21.65 in) is attached to the sled, which is then pulled to the top of the ramp and released to strike the gearbox/rear-impact absorption structure combination.

To replicate the weight of another car, the sled is ballasted to weigh 780 kg (1716 lb). It strikes the gearbox/rear-impact absorption structure combination at a speed of 12 metres per second (39.4 feet per second) – about 45 kph (30 mph) – the same speed as the frontal impact test. FIA regulations stipulate that structural damage must not extend beyond the rear axle line, and that the sled's average deceleration must not exceed 35 G, with a peak value no greater than 60 G for three milliseconds.

A crash simulation known as the 'nose push-off test' simulates an accident in which the nosebox is struck heavily from the side. Only the datum chassis must undergo this test. The intention is to verify that the nosebox will not become detached from the chassis in these circumstances, denuding the car of its most vital energy-absorbing structure. The front aerofoils are strong enough to act as levers in this type of accident, wrenching the nosebox off.

Unlike the frontal and rear impact simulations described earlier, the nose push-off test is a static – as opposed to dynamic – test: that is to say, impact forces are simulated by steady pressure rather than being actually delivered by one object forcibly striking another.

In preparation for the nose push-off test, the chassis is anchored at the engine mounting points to a sturdy tubular-steel framework. An oblong steel pad measuring 30 x 10 cm (11.42 x 3.94 in) is positioned against the chassis, as close as possible to the interface with the nosebox, bracing the chassis firmly against the substantial loadings that are about to be exerted from the opposite side.

A second pad of identical dimensions is then positioned on the opposite side of the nosebox, 55 cm (21.65 in) forward of the front axle line. Unlike the other pad, which is fixed in position, this pad can translate slowly in a lateral direction by means of a worm-drive mechanism, exerting loadings equivalent to a major sideways impact.

The worm drive is equipped with a load cell to measure the lateral forces exerted on the chassis. It is driven slowly into the side of the nosebox until a force of 40 kN (4 tons) has been exerted, and then held for 30 seconds before being slowly eased away.

If this cycle is performed without any evidence of structural failure – cracking of the carbon-composites or damage to the mounting points – the attendant FIA official deems that the chassis has passed the nose push-off test.

The instrumentation for this test comprises an electrical output from the load cell to a nearby computer, from which a graph is produced in real time. If the instrumentation detects that an increase in distortion is occurring independent of a corresponding increase in load (in which case the upward-curving line on the graph descends suddenly), it is clear that a catastrophic failure has occurred, or is about to occur. At this point, the test may be aborted on the instructions of the attendant race-team personnel.

That way, the chassis is preserved for subsequent reinforcement – albeit with a consequent weight increase – and re-test, provided it has not been irreparably damaged.

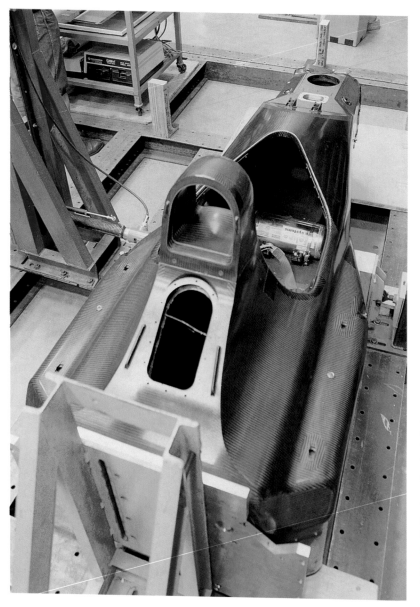

Three different – though comparable – crash scenarios are simulated with a series of static tests known as 'squeeze tests', in which steel pads are employed to compress the chassis laterally, simulating impacts from the side.

Two of the three squeeze tests – the first and the last – employ the same, 30 x 10 cm (11.42 x 3.94 in) pads used for the nose push-off test.

Throughout the squeeze tests, the chassis remains firmly braced at the engine mounting points to prevent any vertical movement – because certain shapes of chassis would have a tendency to pop out from between the pads. The forces are applied by a worm-drive mechanism linked to a load cell. Measurements of deformation are made from *inside* the chassis, which is only deemed to have passed each of the three tests if it withstands the mandatory compression force and springs back to within 1 mm (0.04 in) of its original shape, thereby demonstrating that permanent distortion has not occurred. FIA regulations state that deformation must not exceed 20 mm (0.79 in), but this value is seldom – if ever – recorded, as structural failure would almost certainly have already occurred.

The first of the squeeze tests is applied to a specified point at the front of the chassis, and is designed to assess the structure's ability to resist intrusion into the cockpit footwell by a front wheel/suspension assembly. It is necessary, also, to ensure that the chassis will not collapse inwards under the force of an impact, crushing the driver's feet and ankles. The datum chassis must undergo a compressive force of 25 kN (2.5 tons), while subsequent chassis are exposed to 20 kN (2 tons).

Another squeeze test is applied to a specified point at the middle of the chassis, to assess the ability of the structure to resist a lateral intrusion into the region of the cockpit occupied by the driver's torso. For this test, every single chassis destined for Formula 1 races must undergo a compressive force of 30 kN (3 tons), applied by a steel pad measuring 20 cm (7.88 in) in diameter.

The third and final squeeze test is applied to the rear of the chassis – employing the 30 x 10 cm (11.42 x 3.94 in) pads once again – to assess the ability of the structure to resist a lateral intrusion into the fuel cell compartment, which might puncture the cell itself. The datum chassis must undergo a compressive force of 25 kN (2.5 tons), while subsequent chassis are exposed to 20 kN (2 tons). Loads are applied at the centre of the region in which the fuel cell is housed, because that is the weakest spot.

By far the most significant amendment to the Formula 1 crash-test regulations in the wake of the tragic events of 1994 was the introduction of a 'dynamic side-impact test'. Since the start of the 1995 season, Formula 1 cars have had to incorporate side-impact absorption structures on the chassis flanks.

While most designers have simply incorporated deformable 'bumps' on the sides of the chassis, hidden within the sidepods, some have devised highly innovative structures which protrude very visibly in front of the sidepods and also have an aerodynamic function. The most radical approach is seen on the 1998-model Benetton, the B198: Nick Wirth's first design for the team. Similar structures appeared on the 1995-model Simtek car, which Wirth also designed.

To meet the crash-test criteria, the chassis is fixed sideways-on in a steel frame and supported by a rigid moulding which conforms exactly to the contours of the side of the chassis opposite the side about to be struck. It is impacted by a steel plate measuring 45 x 55 cm (17.72 x 21.65 in), mounted on a pendulum suspended from a tall steel-framework gantry. The pendulum has a parallelogram geometry to ensure that the steel plate strikes at a directly perpendicular angle to the side-impact absorption structure. It strikes at a specified point roughly half-way along the cockpit aperture – with the centre of the plate 27.5 cm (10.83 in) above the base of the chassis – the most vulnerable point in this region.

The impacting mass weighs 780 kg (1716 lb) and strikes at 7 metres per second (22.75 feet per second): about 25 kph (15 mph). The average deceleration of the pendulum-mounted steel plate – as measured by an accelerometer fixed to the back of it – must not exceed 10 G, and damage must be limited to the side-impact absorption structure and not extend to the chassis itself.

Only the datum chassis must undergo this test.

To assess the ability of the chassis to resist intrusion into the underside in the region where the fuel cell is situated, an 'underside impact simulation' is conducted. This is a static test similar to the lateral squeeze tests described above, but the chassis is positioned on its side and the load is applied with a worm-drive mechanism to the underside, using only a single steel plate measuring 20 cm (7.88 in) in diameter.

The chassis, fixed at the engine mounting points, is braced at the rollover hoop against the loads about to be applied from the opposite direction. To pass the test, the datum chassis must withstand a compression force – measured by a load cell – of 12.5 kN (1.25 tons), held for 30 seconds, while subsequent chassis need only withstand a load of 10 kN (1 ton). The permissible limits to deformation are identical to those for the lateral squeeze tests.

Thankfully, rollover accidents – like that survived by Forti driver Luca Badoer in the 1996 Argentine Grand Prix – are rare in Formula 1, but the cars must be capable of protecting their occupants in such circumstances.

A 'rollover impact test' simulates this type of accident. It is a static test, in which a steel plate measuring 20 cm (7.88 in) in diameter, equipped with a load cell, is slowly driven downwards onto the top of the rollover hoop by means of a hydraulic ram.

The chassis is attached at the engine mounting points to a tubular steel platform which is inclined at a nose-up angle, and also canted to one side, in order to replicate the combination of loadings that would typically occur in a rollover accident. Specifically, these loadings would comprise: a lateral component, imparted by the car's rolling motion: a longitudinal component, imparted by the car's forward momentum and exerted either forwards or backwards, depending on the orientation of the car at the moment of impact; and a vertical component, imparted as the car drops down.

A load of 76 kN (7.6 tons) is applied: this translates into 57.39 kN (5.74 tons) vertically, 42.08 kN (4.2 tons) longitudinally, and 11.48 kN (1.15 tons) laterally. The chassis can be heard creaking and groaning in the process. FIA regulations specify that structural deformation must not exceed 50 mm (1.95 in), and must be contained within the top 100 mm (3.9 in) of the rollover hoop.

A follow-up test introduced for the start of the 1998 season involves driving a smaller steel plate – 10 cm (3.94 in) in diameter – onto the area immediately in front of the cockpit aperture: a region which bears internal reinforcement in its carbon-composite construction to perform essentially the same task as a rollover hoop. A load of 75 kN (7.5 tons) is applied, but unlike the first element of the test it is applied squarely onto the car, rather than at an angle.

Only the datum chassis is required to undergo the two elements of this test.

Protecting the driver's cockpit environment is obviously the single most important objective of the crash-test regime. To ensure that the sides of the cockpit offer sufficient protection, and will not collapse downwards under the force of an impact with another object – such as a flying car in a first-corner melee – a 'cockpit rim test' is undertaken.

This is a static test in which two steel plates – each measuring 10 cm (3.94 in) in diameter – are driven slowly down onto either side of the cockpit aperture by a worm drive linked to a load cell. The forces are directed onto specified points roughly half-way along the cockpit opening. A load of 10 kN (1 ton) is applied to the datum chassis: subsequent chassis are exposed to a load of 8 kN (0.8 ton).

The FIA sets the same structural deformation limits for the cockpit rim test as for the earlier lateral squeeze tests and underside impact simulation.

In order to protect the driver's head in a major frontal impact, FIA regulations demand that either the steering wheel should have a deformable structure built into it, or there should be a collapsible steering column. To verify that there is sufficient impact-absorption, a 'steering wheel impact test' is conducted.

This test has similarities to the dynamic chassis side-impact test described earlier, in that the structure to be tested is positioned beneath a pendulum apparatus suspended from a steel-framework gantry. However, instead of the whole chassis being fixed in place, in this case only the components which contribute directly to the test – namely, the key elements of the steering system – are put in place. Also, the rig used for this test is much smaller than the one employed for the dynamic chassis side-impact test, so the pendulum apparatus does not need a parallelogram geometry to deliver the impact load squarely onto the steering wheel.

A hemispherical steel weight of 8 kg (17.64 lb) measuring 165 mm (6.5 in) in diameter and fixed at the end of the pendulum arm is swung at the centre of the steering wheel in the same axis as the steering column. It strikes at a speed of 7 metres per second (22.75 feet per second): about 25 kph (15 mph). To pass the test, the average deceleration of the hemispherical weight – as measured by an accelerometer fixed to the back of it – must not exceed 80 G for more than three milliseconds. Furthermore, the steering wheel must remain capable of being removed in the normal manner to allow the driver to be extracted from the car.

chapter 3 AERODYNAMICS

AERODYNAMICS are the single most important factor in Formula 1 car design. Jordan's chief designer, Gary Anderson, has even gone so far as to state that aerodynamics now account for up to 80 per cent of the car's performance.

In motor racing, aerodynamic efficiency was for decades regarded purely as a means of achieving higher speeds on the straights, but it can also bring profound improvements to cornering and braking performance. The recognition and exploitation of this fact has been the single most important technological development in Formula 1 over the past 30 years.

The aerodynamic devices, in concert with the tyres, endow the modern Formula 1 car with phenomenal cornering ability. Lateral forces of over 3.5 G can be generated through high-speed corners. By comparison, an ordinary roadgoing car cannot sustain a lateral force of much more than 1 G, because at about that point it loses its grip and starts to slide away.

Downforce is the key to this exceptional cornering performance: the creation of 'negative lift' – with aerodynamic devices performing the opposite function to the wings of an aircraft – which presses the car down onto the racetrack surface and increases the grip of the tyres. As well as permitting increased cornering speeds, downforce aids braking performance – again, by increasing tyre-grip.

New regulations introduced for 1998 were aimed at reducing downforce levels in the interests of safety. The reduction in downforce attributable to these regulation-changes was about 15 per cent, but such is the pace of development in Formula 1 that most of this deficit was expected to be clawed back during the course of that season.

Most of a Formula 1 car's aerodynamic aids are composed of two skins of carbonfibre sandwiching a layer of aluminium honeycomb material. They are produced by essentially the same process of pattern-making, mould-making and laying-up as was described for the manufacture of the chassis in Chapter 1.

A Formula 1 car is, in essence, a 'dirty' shape aerodynamically – because FIA regulations require single-seaters to have open bodywork, with the wheels exposed rather than faired in – so the challenge of achieving high levels of aerodynamic efficiency is a considerable one.

Although the racetrack is the ultimate proving ground, the windtunnel is where this challenge is met.

An exquisitely detailed scale model, in which every relevant feature of the full-sized car is faithfully reproduced, is created for windtunnel testing. Most of the windtunnels employed for Formula 1 testing accommodate 40- to 50-per cent scale models. During the course of testing, dozens of bolt-on modifications are tried to see if they improve performance: alternatively shaped noseboxes, rear diffusers, sidepod air intakes, front and rear aerofoils and so forth. Aerodynamic effects in different regions of the car tend to be interrelated, so the process is a complex one. Aerodynamicists are also aware that external factors will influence the performance of their car: a gust of wind, or the turbulent air produced by the car in front.

The top teams have up to five aerodynamicists on-strength, because there are so many factors to consider.

Windtunnel testing is not limited to the gestation period of a new car – although that is certainly when the workload is most concentrated. It continues during the course of the season, as refinements are developed in the endless search for better performance.

There is much more to a windtunnel than first meets the eye. Published photographs of windtunnels in operation usually show the windtunnel model suspended from a streamlined strut in the area known as the working section, but that is but one small part of the overall facility. Out of sight, a huge fan impels the flow of air which passes over the model. The air travels a considerable distance to reach the working section. It is accelerated just before it gets there by the walls, floor and ceiling converging to form what is termed a contraction nozzle.

After exiting the working section, the airflow is recirculated back through the fan to pass over the model time after time. This ensures consistent test results, because if fresh air was drawn from outside it would introduce temperature fluctuations, altering its density unpredictably.

To simulate actual conditions as accurately as possible, the windtunnel model is suspended above a moving belt which simulates the relative movement of the racetrack surface beneath the car's wheels. The 'moving ground', as it is called, is akin to a conveyor belt and moves at a speed which corresponds with the speed of the airflow passing through the windtunnel – again, to accurately simulate actual conditions.

The four wheel/tyre units are not actually fixed to the windtunnel model. Instead, they are positioned a fractional distance away from it – individually supported on horizontal struts mounted on either side of the moving belt – and they rest on the belt, which rotates them at a proportionate speed. This arrangement allows the drag levels on each wheel/tyre unit to be independently measured.

Due to their large size – and uncompromising shape! – the tyres create appreciable drag: around one-third of the car's total drag. Aerodynamicists wish to assess how tyre drag levels are influenced by changes made to other parts of the car.

The streamlined strut from which the model is suspended is part of a complex system which measures the major aerodynamic forces acting on the model. The resulting data are fed to a computer in the windtunnel control room, overlooking the working section. Aerodynamicists place particular emphasis on three parameters: downforce, drag and balance.

Downforce levels should be increased during the course of a sustained windtunnel testing programme as a result of modifications made to the model through constant experimentation. It is necessary to have an elaborate suction system immediately below the working section to keep the moving belt uniformly flat, because – despite its modest size – the scale racing car generates considerable downforce and would otherwise draw parts of the belt up towards it.

Drag levels play a critical part in aerodynamic performance, because drag not only impairs the car's speed potential, but also degrades its fuel economy. Aerodynamicists attempt to increase downforce whilst not increasing drag.

Balance, as the term applies to racing car aerodynamics, means the car's sensitivity to changes in pitch and heave. Changes in pitch occur when the car pitches nose-up under acceleration or nose-down under braking; these cause the car's centre of pressure to shift fore and aft, which destabilises it. Key objectives of windtunnel testing are to both minimise this centre-of-pressure shift and improve the car's tolerance to shifts when they occur. Changes in heave are vertical translations – changes in ride-height – as the car passes over undulations in the racetrack surface; these also destabilise the car, because they cause its downforce levels to vary unpredictably. Computer-controlled servos can alter the model's pitch angle and ride-height remotely while the windtunnel is in operation, allowing aerodynamicists to assess the effects such movements have on the car's balance.

Most of the Formula 1 teams have their own windtunnels. Jordan, for example, built its windtunnel in 1997 at a cost of £2.7 million. However, some teams undertake their windtunnel testing at other facilities. For example, McLaren has an exclusive agreement to use the windtunnel operated by the National Maritime Institution at Teddington near London, and the Tyrrell team – which had previously hired windtunnel facilities at the University of Southampton at a cost of around £1500 per day – finally got its own facility operating at Bournemouth International Airport in early 1998, sharing it in a joint venture with sponsor European Aviation.

The amount of windtunnel testing a team undertakes varies according to whether it has its own windtunnel, or has to share testing time with the windtunnel owner or other users of a proprietary windtunnel, in which case availability and budgetary limitations can come into play. The total amount of windtunnel time undertaken in the course of a year varies from a minimum of around 50 days to a maximum of around 150.

Distance is no object when the need for a windtunnel is urgent. The Stewart team, when it was gearing up to enter Formula 1 at the start of 1997 with limited facilities of its own, conducted its windtunnel testing an ocean and a continent away, at the Swift facility in San Clemente, California.

The Stewart team is run by triple World Drivers' Champion Jackie Stewart and his son Paul, and is heavily supported by the Ford Motor Company. Based in Milton Keynes, just north of London, it had a very promising debut season – highlighted by an excellent second-place finish by Rubens Barrichello in the Monaco Grand Prix. Although the Stewart looks conventional externally, design chief Alan Jenkins is an adventurous innovator.

The front aerofoils typically provide about 25 per cent of the car's total downforce – but a car following another closely can lose as much as 30 per cent of that downforce, because the turbulence created by the car in front diminishes its aerodynamic efficiency. This is the main reason why overtaking has become a comparatively rare occurrence in Formula 1.

It was explained in the Introduction to this book that designers attempt to bring weight forward as much as possible, because the car's heaviest components – the engine, gearbox and fuel load – are unavoidably concentrated at the rear, placing a proportionately greater burden on the rear tyres. But aside from the favourable effect on weight distribution, there is also an *aerodynamic* benefit to transferring weight onto the front tyres.

This is because, with more weight placed on the rear tyres, more rear downforce is required to maintain cornering performance, which in turn creates a higher level of aerodynamic drag. It is preferable, therefore, to redistribute weight to the front, then generate additional downforce with the front aerofoils to deal with it, as this creates a better overall balance.

Each front aerofoil assembly is usually composed of either two or three aerofoil elements. They are usually mounted on two streamlined struts beneath the nosebox, but a single-strut arrangement has been seen on occasion. On some cars with a two-strut mounting arrangement, the struts are diagonal or arched rather than vertical to contribute additional lateral rigidity.

At the extremities of the front aerofoils are the endplates. These channel the airflow for maximum efficiency, by preventing it from 'spilling out' from the ends of the aerofoil elements and diminishing their effectiveness. They also help to smooth the flow of air around the front tyres. The airflow, as it departs the front aerofoil assembly and passes under the car, must be smooth and well-directed if the undertray and rear diffuser are to perform well.

The clearance between the front aerofoil assembly and the racetrack surface can be adjusted, as can the angles of the individual aerofoil elements. The greater the angle, the greater the downforce generated.

To increase downforce, most cars have a 'Gurney-flap' fitted to the trailing edge of the front aerofoil assembly. Named after the legendary American racing driver Dan Gurney, this is a thin strip of carbonfibre which adds a small lip to the aerofoil shape, increasing the downforce it generates (these devices are also fitted to the rear aerofoils and into the rear diffuser). When even more front downforce is required, some cars have two extra aerofoils mounted above the main aerofoil assembly. These 'moustache' winglets were first introduced by the Tyrrell team.

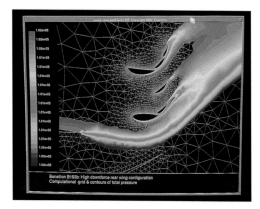

Benetton B193b: High downforce rear wing configuration
Computational grid & contours of total pressure

Continuing advances in technology are altering the nature of aerodynamic testing. In the windtunnel, laser beams are now being used to 'visualise' turbulence and to measure the airflow at specific points. Lasers offer the benefit of being able to accurately measure the characteristics of the airflow without physically interfering with it.

Also, windtunnel testing is being increasingly complemented by computer-based analysis of airflow behaviour. An emerging branch of science known as Computational Fluid Dynamics (CFD) allows the aerodynamic performance of particular shapes to be predicted before a windtunnel model is actually built. CFD also allows comparisons to be made with the results of physically testing models in the windtunnel, in order to increase the accuracy of testing techniques.

As with the FEA structural analysis technique described in Chapter 1, the results of CFD analyses are presented in a colour-coded form which simplifies interpretation.

Mounting the front aerofoil assembly closer to the racetrack surface would increase its efficiency, but there are regulations limiting how close it can be. In 1993, the FIA raised the mandatory minimum clearance between the front aerofoil endplates and the racetrack surface to 40 mm (1.54 in). It had previously been 25 mm (1 in).

In 1997, Ferrari introduced a front aerofoil constructed with a special carbonfibre lay-up which caused it to flex downwards at the ends under the influence of aerodynamic loads. In doing so, it closed the gap between the endplates and the racetrack surface, increasing its efficiency without creating more drag. When the car was at rest, without any aerodynamic influence, the Ferrari's front aerofoil ground clearance met the FIA's minimum requirement. But a mere push of the hand at its extremities was enough to make it bend down – whereas, normally, several people could stand on each side without it bending perceptibly.

The FIA regulations prohibit 'movable aerodynamic devices' – everything with an aerodynamic influence must be fixed in place while the car is in motion – but this had generally been interpreted as a prohibition on *mechanical* methods of altering the position and/or angle of aerodynamic aids. The regulations did not actually specify how *stiff* a wing must be, so this was a loophole designers could exploit. Ferrari had interpreted the regulations to the letter, rather than the spirit: a common situation in Formula 1.

All structures flex to some extent under load – whether it is the wing of an aircraft or the shaft of a tennis racket. If they were too stiff they would break. Ferrari's innovative front aerofoil, with a pronounced flexing capability deliberately designed in, posed problems for Formula 1's legislators. In the predominantly American-based CART Championship, which features cars with many similarities to Formula 1 cars, officials hang weights from specified areas of bodywork – including the aerofoils – and then take measurements to ensure that flexing has not exceeded certain prescribed limits.

This solution was adopted by the FIA for Formula 1 in 1998.

First seen at a Grand Prix in 1994, barge-boards – also known as turning vanes – are mounted on the sides of Formula 1 cars to help control the complex disturbances in the airflow departing the front aerofoils. If left unchecked, these disturbances would diminish the efficiency of the other aerodynamic devices situated further back on the car.

New regulations for 1998 have resulted in the front wheels being moved into the airflow controlled by the barge-boards, so their role has become even more important.

Different sizes, shapes and combinations of barge-boards are fitted according to the aerodynamic requirements of particular cars at particular circuits, and there have to be slots in the barge-boards in certain configurations to allow elements of the front suspension to pass through. Some barge-boards are low and elongated, extending as far back as the sidepod openings, while others are tall and truncated.

Elongated barge-boards are pictured fitted to the 1997-model Minardi. This little team from Faenza in Italy has survived an ultra-competitive era of Formula 1 which has seen more illustrious names, such as Brabham and Lotus, disappear. It lacks the budget, and therefore technical facilities, of the front-running teams – but has performed admirably and launched the careers of several top drivers, including Giancarlo Fisichella.

Giancarlo Minardi's cars are the product of chief designer Gustav Brunner, working under technical director Gabriele Tredozzi.

The trend towards high noses in Formula 1 – started by Tyrrell design chief Harvey Postlethwaite – was driven by a desire to allow as much air as possible to get underneath the car, where it can be harnessed by the under-tray and rear diffuser to generate extra downforce. The nose of the 1998-model Ferrari is so high that it has two protrusions on its underside to accommodate recesses for the driver's heels.

McLaren driver David Coulthard famously likened the current driving posture to lying in a bath and exercising control with one's feet on the taps!

Pronounced humps on the noses of some cars are intended to direct airflow around the cockpit and into the airbox.

McLaren's technical director, Adrian Newey, is universally acknowledged as the most talented designer in Formula 1. His brilliance, enshrined in the 1998-model MP4/13, has allowed team boss Ron Dennis to finally re-establish McLaren as the pre-eminent force in Grand Prix racing.

The Formula 1 car's most important aerodynamic device is virtually invisible to the spectator – unless the car is being hoisted high into the air on a crane! It is the undertray: a panel of carbonfibre/aluminium honeycomb sandwich construction, with three flat surfaces – a central 'keel' with an elevated surface on either side – which is attached directly to the underside of the chassis.

In 1978, the Lotus Formula 1 cars designed by Colin Chapman achieved astronomical success by embodying an entirely new concept for generating downforce. The cars had large aerofoils mounted within their sidepods, and sliding 'skirts' to seal the gap between the sides of the car and the racetrack surface to increase the effectiveness of these aerofoils. The revolutionary Lotus – deemed thoroughly legal – was universally copied, and ushered in what became known as the 'ground effects' era of Formula 1 car design.

That era came to an end in 1983, when the so-called 'flat bottom' regulation was introduced in order to reduce downforce and thereby limit the cornering speeds of Formula 1 cars, which by then had become dangerously high. While this regulation prevents designers from incorporating any contoured features into the undertray to create downforce, it leaves them free to introduce a virtually unlimited amount of profiling into the rear diffuser – the upward-sloping aerodynamic device located immediately aft of the undertray.

The relationship between the undertray and the rear diffuser is crucial. The diffuser's upward-sloping shape widens the gap between the underside of the car and the racetrack surface, which causes the airflow there to slow down in the same way that the flow of water slows down when a river becomes wider. When an airflow slows down its pressure increases, so this causes it to be expelled more rapidly from the back of the diffuser. This draws air from beneath the undertray, accelerating it, and as the airflow there accelerates its pressure decreases – creating downforce which sucks the car onto the racetrack surface.

The new regulations introduced for 1998 stipulated that the cars had to be 20 cm (7.88 in) – ten per cent – narrower than before: the maximum permissible track was reduced from 200 cm (78.8 in) to 180 cm (70.92 in). The teams responded by moving the wheels closer to the car, by shortening the suspension, rather than reducing the body width of the car itself, as that would have reduced the area of the undertray and cost downforce. Nevertheless, the rear wheels now encroached into the zone occupied by the rear diffuser – reducing its area by about 25 per cent – so there was an inevitable loss of downforce.

Sculpted around the gearbox casing, the rear diffuser actually comprises several short tunnels which occupy virtually all of the space between the rear wheels. 'Splitters' in the rear diffuser channel the airflow to maximum effect: their shapes and positions are determined by relentless windtunnel testing. Like the undertray, the rear diffuser has a carbonfibre/aluminium honeycomb sandwich construction. Although it is an extension of the undertray, it is mounted on the rear-impact absorption structure, which is itself fixed to the gearbox.

At the front of the undertray, in the centre, there is a vertical 'splitter' which diverts the air to either side and under the car.

During windtunnel testing, aerodynamicists 'tune' the length of the undertray in concert with changes they make to the shape of the rear diffuser. Their aim is to achieve the optimum – as opposed to the maximum – level of downforce, because designers are also concerned with the aerodynamic balance of the car, seeking to engender stability by alleviating the unsettling effects of braking, accelerating and negotiating undulations in the racetrack surface.

The precise position where the exhaust pipes protrude into the rear diffuser region is determined by the team's aerodynamicists during windtunnel testing. This is because the input of high-energy exhaust gases into this region, which is very sensitive aerodynamically, can have a critical influence on the car's stability – and, if not properly catered for, would generate enough extra downforce to cause the car to pitch unpredictably when the driver lifts his foot off the throttle pedal! The ends of the exhaust pipes are angled upwards, and are positioned above the rear diffuser on some cars and below it on others.

So critical is the interplay between the exhaust gases and the rear diffuser that compressed air is fed through scale reproductions of the exhaust pipes during windtunnel testing to replicate the aerodynamic effects as accurately as possible, and FIA regulations now class the exhaust pipes as part of the car's aerodynamics. Several teams have gone so far as to alter the positioning of the square high-intensity rear light – which the driver turns on in conditions of poor visibility – in order to improve the flow of air and exhaust gases in that region. Due to its safety function, the siting of this light is governed by FIA regulations, but tilting it through 45 degrees is deemed entirely legal and effectively raises its lower corners further out of the airflow.

Among the many factors which must be considered when refining the aerodynamics in this region is ensuring that the hot exhaust gases will not damage elements of the rear suspension.

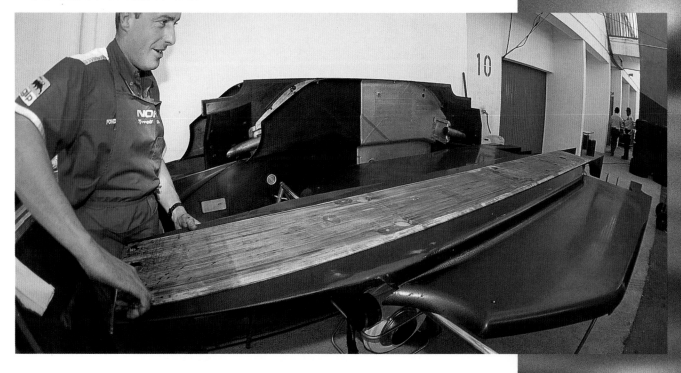

Because higher levels of downforce permit higher cornering speeds, the FIA has repeatedly introduced measures to restrict it on safety grounds. For the start of the 1994 season, the FIA introduced a new regulation to force teams to run their cars with a greater amount of ground clearance – reducing the effectiveness of the under-tray/rear diffuser combination in creating downforce. The regulation demanded that the undertray be fitted with a strip of Jabroc wood 10 mm (0.4 in) thick. If that wooden strip was found to be less than 9 mm (0.36 in) thick at the end of a race, it would be assumed that the car in question had run at an illegally low ride-height, and it would therefore be disqualified from the results.

In 1994, when accidents on two consecutive days claimed the lives of Roland Ratzenberger and Ayrton Senna at Italy's Imola circuit, the FIA hurriedly introduced regulations which would restrict the speed of the cars in corners still further. Again, downforce levels were targeted: a restriction was placed on the length of the rear diffuser.

For the start of the 1995 season, the FIA introduced the so-called 'stepped bottom' regulation to reduce downforce levels yet again. This required the undertray to have two raised 'steps' 50 mm (1.95 in) high, one on either side, significantly increasing the clearance between most of the undertray and the racetrack surface by converting what had previously been the single 'flat bottom' created by the 1983 regulation into the far less effective three-surface, two-level structure we see today.

What then became the central 'keel' of the undertray still had to carry a 10-mm (0.4-in) strip of Jabroc, so the actual increase in ride-height resulting from the new 'stepped bottom' regulation was 60 mm (2.35 in) for all but the central section immediately beneath the chassis, which remained at the original height.

Such is the determination and ingenuity of Formula 1 designers in the face of all these restrictions that the original downforce levels have been largely regained over the intervening period. However, the increases in ride-height have deprived enthusiasts of the spectacle of showers of sparks being cast from the titanium skids which were previously fitted to the undertray and front aerofoil endplates to protect them from damage when the car 'bottomed out' with a heavy fuel load.

The sidepods house the radiator ducts and 'fill' much of the space between the front and rear wheels with a streamlined structure. The design process required to define the shape of the sidepods is a good example of the way in which aerodynamic effects in different regions of the car tend to be interrelated, complicating the process considerably. In determining the height of the sidepods, for example, a compromise must be made because they must be tall enough to accommodate the radiators, but they must not be so tall as to interfere with the flow of air over the upper elements of the rear aerofoil assembly.

Sidepod height also influences the flow of air over the car as a whole. The airflow, having passed over the front tyres, must transit the upper surfaces of the sidepods before passing over the rear tyres. The sidepod height has a bearing on the manner in which the airflow changes direction over those three regions, which in turn has a bearing on the total downforce generated by the car, and on its stability.

The length of the undertray directly influences the length of the sidepods, due to an FIA regulation known as the 'shadowplate ruling'. This stipulates that the sidepods must not extend beyond the perimeter of the under-tray, as viewed from above. Yet the length, height and shape of the sidepods have a bearing on the total lift-to-drag ratio of the car – which is a critical factor – so, again, a compromise must be made at the design stage.

The shape of the sidepod air intakes is important, and is determined by windtunnel testing. It is necessary to achieve the smoothest possible flow of air into the intakes, or the radiators will not be able to perform efficiently. The 1998-model Prost AP01 has very sharp edges to its sidepod intakes. In addition, the Prost AP01 features gracefully streamlined 'bumps' in front of the sidepods which serve a dual purpose. They are side-impact deformable structures, but they also have an aerodynamic function, helping to feed air into the radiators and channelling the airflow under the car and along its flanks.

Formed from what was originally the Ligier team, the Prost equipe – run by quadruple World Drivers' Champion Alain Prost – is based in a new factory at Guyoncourt near Paris, having previously resided at the Magny-Cours racetrack in central France. The team's chief designer is Loic Bigois.

Housed within the sidepods are the carbonfibre radiator ducts. Their shape – which is determined by windtunnel testing – must be such that the airflow remains smooth on its journey to the radiators. If it becomes turbulent, there will not be an even distribution of cooling air across the full face of each radiator core and the engine will have a tendency to overheat.

Oversizing the radiators to compensate for any deficiencies in the radiator duct design is an unacceptable compromise, because additional radiator area incurs additional aerodynamic drag, as well as excess weight.

When a driver makes an accidental excursion into one of the trackside gravel traps, copious quantities of gravel are scooped into the radiator ducts. If the driver is fortunate and skilful enough to regain the circuit, there is a surprise in store. The first time he depresses the brake pedal heavily, a torrent of gravel is thrown out onto the track in front of him.

Achieving a smooth flow of air into the airbox, so that the engine can perform to maximum efficiency, is a key objective. Various attempts are made to funnel turbulent air from around the driver's helmet away, in order to allow only 'clean' air into the airbox.

Reducing the levels of turbulence around the driver's helmet has become a priority in recent years – not only because it can diminish the quality of the airflow into the engine, but also because the effects of the airflow can upset a driver's concentration. 'Trip strips' and other sculpted features on the helmet – all perfected in the windtunnel – now reduce its tendency to lift at high speeds, and smooth out the airflow around the helmet to reduce buffeting.

Some cars have a vestigial Perspex windscreen or a low-line carbonfibre fairing around the front of the cockpit opening for the same purpose.

In 1997, Ferrari experimented with two long strakes, each mounted at a 45-degree angle, fitted along the length of the car from the cockpit forwards. About 10 cm (3.85 in) high and 3.5 cm (1.4 in) thick, they were intended to reduce the buffeting driver Eddie Irvine was complaining of, and to improve the flow of air into the airbox.

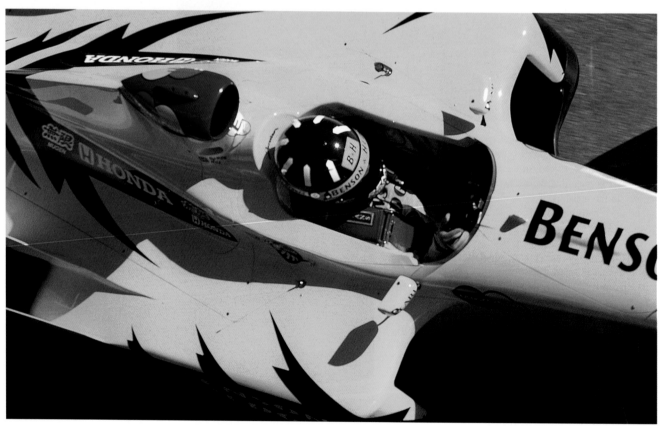

Mesmerising views from on-board cameras – housed in streamlined aluminium fairings which cause minimal aerodynamic disturbance – have transformed the public perception of Formula 1. By regulation, each car must carry at least two cameras – or dummies of the same weight – one of which must be mounted atop the rollover hoop. The resulting images are seen not only by tens of millions of TV viewers around the world, but also by tens of thousands of spectators at the circuit when they appear on gigantic track-side screens.

Within each streamlined fairing, the camera itself occupies only a very small space: most of the fairing is occupied by a transmitter and a telemetry data receiver. A strip of clear film spools past the lens, keeping the picture free of dead insects, oil and other accumulating deposits.

All of the cameras are supplied by the Formula One Constructors Association (FOCA). They transmit their pictures via a helicopter flying above the circuit. At any given race, although all the cars carry cameras, only pictures from three at any one time are transmitted to the global TV feed. FOCA maintains two-way communication with the cameras, turning the units on and off, and operating their lens-cleaner mechanisms.

To increase downforce, additional aerofoils are often fitted to the cars. The Hungarian Grand Prix, with its multiplicity of mid-speed corners, typically sees the greatest number of aerodynamic appendages added to cars in an effort to augment downforce.

Faced with the major loss of downforce which resulted from the regulation-changes for 1994 and 1995, some teams exploited a loophole in the regulations governing the dimensions of protruberances amidships by mounting additional aerofoils in that region. The first was McLaren, which mounted a single winglet atop the engine cover on its 1995-model car (Jordan followed suit with a similar design the following year), then Minardi responded with a novel variation: a winglet cantilevered out from the leading edge of the rear aerofoil assembly. The loophole allowed these winglets to be mounted higher than the rear aerofoil assembly, so their presence did not degrade the quality of the air passing to that.

By far the most exotic winglet arrangement – exploiting a similar loophole – was the Tyrrell team's outlandish 'X-wing' concept: a high-downforce configuration which appeared at many Grands Prix in 1997, in which winglets were mounted on struts high above the car.

Tyrrell has established a reputation for innovation, particularly in the realm of aerodynamics. No-one who saw them will ever forget the radical six-wheelers the team deployed in 1976 and 1977. With four tiny wheels at the front, the intention was to reduce the car's frontal area – and thereby reduce aerodynamic drag – whilst at the same time increasing the braking capability. The cars scored several triumphs, including a fantastic one-two finish in the Swedish Grand Prix, but the six-wheel arrangement was inevitably heavier than a conventional layout, so the theoretical benefits were literally outweighed.

FIA regulations now limit the number of wheels on Formula 1 cars to four.

Unable to emulate its multiple World Championship successes with Jackie Stewart at the wheel in the late 1960s and early 1970s, Tyrrell has now been absorbed into the new 'superteam' formed by top CART Champ Car manufacturer Reynard and Jacques Villeneuve's manager, Craig Pollock, funded by tobacco giant BAT. It will make its debut in 1999.

Although it has a very functional purpose – which is to house the engine air inlet duct, the engine, the gearbox and the rear suspension – the engine cover also serves a key aerodynamic role. It must be as streamlined as possible, in order to allow the airflow to pass smoothly to the rear aerofoil assembly. And it must also have the minimum frontal area in order to reduce drag.

The engine cover sweeps down to hug the contours of the highest points on the engine and the gearbox-mounted suspension elements, terminating at the base of the mounting for the rear aerofoil assembly. At the sides, it flares out gracefully to meet the sidepods.

In 1997, Renault and Williams worked together to develop a very small engine air inlet duct, which made it possible to create a very low engine cover and thereby improve the aerodynamic efficiency at the back of the car.

The engine cover pictured here belongs to a Benetton. The Enstone, Oxfordshire-based team has not been able to repeat the championship-winning successes of its 'Schumacher Era', but it is one of the best-financed, best-equipped campaigners in Formula 1 and – with the organisational genius of David Richards – it cannot be long before the glory days return.

The airflow around the rear tyres must be carefully controlled if the car is to be aerodynamically efficient. At the rear of the car, the sides curve inwards Coke bottle-style to control the airflow around the inner surfaces of the rear tyres and thereby reduce drag and maximise the efficiency of the rear diffuser. These features are called 'scallops'.

Graceful extensions of the upper-rear sections of the sidepods generate additional downforce and assist the airflow's passage over the rear tyres. These are known as 'flip-ups'.

In 1997, most cars had winglets mounted on the outer sides of the rear aerofoil endplates, immediately in front of the rear tyres, to generate extra downforce. In fact, only Williams and Stewart *didn't* have these winglets that year – but they were banned for 1998 under the FIA's new measures to reduce downforce, so aerodynamic 'flip-ups' became the only alternative.

The rear aerofoil assembly is capable of generating up to one-third of the car's total downforce. It can be made up of a multiplicity of aerofoils – in 1997 some cars ran with up to four tiers of aerofoils – or it can have a 'minimal' configuration.

This is because the amount of downforce required varies from one racetrack to another, and a compromise must be struck between downforce and maximum speed. The German Grand Prix, held at the super-fast Hockenheim circuit – where the cars spend about 75 per cent of the lap at full throttle – traditionally sees teams running as little aerofoil area and angle as possible to maximise the speed on the long straights.

However, the superior power of some engines has allowed certain teams to set greater aerofoil angles – thereby increasing cornering speeds and reducing braking distances – and still reach the same high top speeds.

All aerofoil elements are individually adjustable. Two tiers is the usual configuration, and the lower element has pronounced anhedral contouring on some cars. The lower or lowest aerofoil can directly influence the performance of the rear diffuser/undertray combination, so aerodynamicists must attempt to understand the complex interplay between them.

Like the front aerofoil endplates, the rear aerofoil endplates channel the airflow for maximum efficiency by preventing it from 'spilling out' from the ends of the aerofoil elements and diminishing their effectiveness. However, in this case they also serve as the means of mounting the aerofoils onto the car. Some cars have a single column supporting the rear wing assembly – for example, the 1998-model Ferrari and Benetton – while others have two supports.

On some cars the rear endplates are flat, while on others they are dramatically sculpted. In all cases they are composed of two skins of carbonfibre sandwiching a layer of aluminium honeycomb material.

chapter 4 ENGINE & TRANSMISSION

A FORMULA 1 car has around ten times the horsepower of an average family hatchback, but only half the weight. This power-to-weight ratio, combined with the most advanced automotive technology, translates into breathtaking performance.

Formula 1 engines typically have around 900 moving parts, and run at speeds as high as 17,500 rpm – generating around 730–770 hp. At full throttle, the pistons are subjected to acceleration forces of up to 8500 G. On high-speed circuits, the engine can be operating at full throttle for up to 75 per cent of the lap – the car reaching peak speeds as high as 350 kph (215 mph).

Internal surfaces within the engine can reach temperatures of over 300 degrees C. The engine oil and water normally operate at temperatures around 95 degrees C, but in extreme conditions they can soar to 110 degrees C.

It goes without saying that Formula 1 engines are highly stressed! Not surprisingly, the spectacular sight of an engine expiring in a gigantic plume of smoke is one that is seen frequently.

Although there was very little left in this one, a Formula 1 engine normally holds around 10 litres (18 pints) of oil, of which around 7 litres (12 pints) will be within the crankcase and cylinders at any given time. All Formula 1 engines have dry-sump lubrication systems. High-capacity pumps change the oil every 15 seconds.

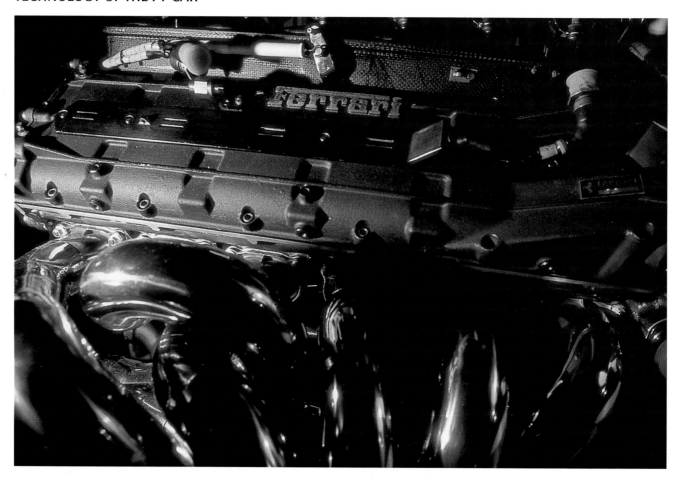

The Ferrari engine – pictured here – is the product of a team which, uniquely, has always manufactured its own powerplants. The other Formula 1 teams obtain their motive power from beyond their own four walls, usually by entering into partnership with a major automobile manufacturer such as Mercedes-Benz or Peugeot – although independent racing engine manufacturers, such as Brian Hart, can also find a place in this rarified corporate climate. In every case, the engines are leased to teams – rather than donated or sold outright – in order to protect the confidentiality of sensitive technology.

Major automobile manufacturers usually supply engines free of charge to their partners. They enter a relationship with a team in order to pursue their marketing and research-and-development objectives. Despite its esteemed status, this can also be said of Ferrari – and of its parent organisation, the mighty Fiat empire, which benefits by association. Independent engine manufacturers, on the other hand, tend to enter into more straight-forward commercial relationships.

Ferrari's 1998-model F300 is the team's first car in four years to be designed entirely in Italy. Previously, design work for the Maranello stable was concentrated in England under John Barnard.

Formula 1 engine designers are only too aware that the engine alone does not win a race – the overall package of car and engine working in harmony does. And it is not simply outright horsepower which singles out a superior engine, because that is only one of several key performance parameters which must be perfected. Of equal importance is the 'driveability' – the ability of the engine to be tractable in a race situation, so that the driver can accelerate cleanly out of slow corners, tiptoe around them when the track conditions are treacherously wet, and jockey for position when he is surrounded by other cars and his ideal racing line has been compromised.

The *installation* of the engine in the car must also be perfected – partly due to the role the engine plays in the overall weight-distribution of the car, but particularly due to its influence on the aerodynamics at the rear of the car. Engine designers make strenuous efforts to keep the engine as compact as possible, so that it leaves more room for the rear diffuser: the upward-sloping 'ramp' at the rear of the undertray which generates so much vital downforce.

Structurally, too, the engine plays a vital role in the overall effectiveness of the car. Formula 1 engines are cantilevered out from the rear wall of the chassis as a fully stressed structural member – carrying the gearbox, to which the rear suspension and rear aerofoil assemblies are in turn attached – so they must be very strong and rigid to cope with the enormous structural loads, yet also extremely lightweight. The engine is mounted as low on the chassis as possible, to help maintain the car's low centre-of-gravity. To marry the engine to the chassis, there are usually a pair of steel or titanium mountings on the sump and either one or two mountings on each camcover.

Fuel economy is another vital factor in engine design. A thirsty engine consumes more time on pitstops, carries more weight, and forces more restrictions on race strategy.

Finally – and most importantly of all – the engine must be reliable. An engine alone cannot win a race, but it can most certainly lose one...

The three foundations of the Formula 1 engine regulations are the 3-litre maximum capacity – reduced from 3.5 litres in 1995 – the requirement that engines be normally aspirated, and the provision for refuelling during the course of the race. The FIA has promised that the stability of the current regulations will be maintained until 2001, but it is likely that these three fundamentals will stand firm until at least 2005.

When embarking on the design of a Formula 1 engine with a clean sheet of paper, the first steps are to select the bore and stroke, and the number of cylinders: eight, ten, or – the maximum permitted by the FIA – 12. A series of computer simulations is undertaken to assess the advantages and disadvantages of all three cylinder configurations in the light of the prevailing regulations and trends. There are too many variables to ensure totally accurate predictions, but the simulations do provide a close enough approximation to permit comparisons on key parameters such as fuel consumption, weight, length, and heat-rejection characteristics.

A key to getting more power from an engine is enabling it to run at higher revs. Running at twice as many revs *theoretically* creates twice as much power, because there are twice as many power strokes. But, in fact, this is not a linear process, because, as the revs increase, the mechanical losses resulting from friction between the moving parts, and minute distortions of components under the increased loads being imposed upon them, increase *more* rapidly. So a point of diminishing returns is reached and the power curve plateaus – and, in any case, the risk of a breakage increases drastically as that point is reached.

The bore exceeds the stroke in all Formula 1 engines, because shorter-stroke engines have the ability to rev higher. Having a shorter stroke also reduces the length of the conrods, making them less susceptible to breakages.

Computer-simulation exercises to determine the best configuration for a new engine are usually conducted in close collaboration with the car manufacturer – and sudden rule-changes have been known to cause difficulties to both parties in the past, which is why the stability of the engine regulations is considered so important by car and engine manufacturers alike.

For example, when Cosworth introduced its new V8 Ford engine in 1994, it was not as the result of an unimaginative 'Ford-Cosworth *always* make V8s for Formula 1 – why change?' mindset, as some pundits asserted. Rather, it was the result of a painstaking study undertaken in close conjunction with the Benetton team, which – after careful analysis of the simulations – concluded that an eight-cylinder arrangement would be the preferred configuration, narrowly superior to a ten-cylinder arrangement at every circuit except super-fast Hockenheim and Monza.

However, the FIA radically altered the regulations during the design and build process for that engine, with refuelling being introduced in an attempt to add more spice to the racing – instantly switching the balance back in favour of a ten-cylinder arrangement. As a general principle, the greater the number of cylinders, the greater the fuel consumption – because the engine's efficiency decreases. Before the introduction of refuelling, the weight of the car at the start-line had been a major factor, and a V8 engine – with its lower fuel consumption – offered the advantage of a lighter fuel load at that critical point in the race (the penalty of carrying a large fuel load is not just the physical weight of the fuel itself, but also the secondary effect of needing 'a larger car' in order to hold the extra fuel).

With race refuelling now permitted – and a full fuel load therefore no longer needing to be carried at the start-line – a key advantage of the V8 simply evaporated (although Benetton-Ford team leader Michael Schumacher *did* win the Drivers' World Championship with this engine that year).

Today, with refuelling thoroughly entrenched in Formula 1 race strategy, V10 engines are universal – this configuration having proved to be the best compromise for a 3-litre unit under the current conditions. As well as offering several advantages in performance over a V8 configuration, a V10 lends itself well to packaging in a chassis designed to the current rules, whereas a 12-cylinder engine is a little too long and heavy to make the slight power advantage it offers worthwhile, and also tends to be inherently less rigid, structurally, as a result of that extra length.

The reason why 'more cylinders' normally means 'more power' is because the engine can rev higher – due to the fact that smaller pistons and conrods have less mass – and there is a greater total valve area, so more air can

be inducted. As with most aspects of engineering, however, there is a downside, because more cylinders means more moving components, and that in turn means greater mechanical losses from factors such as friction. That extra friction also creates more heat within the engine, which must then be dissipated by having larger water and oil radiators – which not only creates extra aerodynamic drag, but also increases the weight of the car, because extra water and oil must be carried.

A jewel among Formula 1 engines is the entirely new Mercedes-Benz unit, introduced at the start of the 1998 season. Mercedes works arm-in-arm with the British-based engine specialist Ilmor to exclusively supply the McLaren team (Ilmor design guru Mario Illien is pictured with the 1997-model McLaren). Mercedes has resurrected the legendary 'Silver Arrows' motif established by the German manufacturer when works team drivers Caracciola, Lang and others annihilated all opposition in the 1930s, and reinforced by the triumphant successes of Fangio and Moss in the mid-1950s.

Mercedes' current contract with McLaren is for five years, terminating at the end of 1999.

In 1997, Formula 1 supremo Bernie Ecclestone – perhaps fearing a shortage of good powerplants in the future – proposed that engine manufacturers should be obligated to supply two teams, just as engine manufacturers in the American CART Championship are required to supply a minimum number of cars. His proposal met with a swift rebuff from the manufacturers – most vociferously Mercedes, whose motorsport chief Norbert Haug countered, 'We are trying to create a new image of the "Silver Arrows", so we can't have a "Blue Arrows" or a "Red Arrows".'

As well as serving its own needs, Ferrari supplies engines to the Swiss-based Sauber team, for a reputed US$15 million annual leasing fee. Although essentially the same engine as that installed in the factory Ferraris, it is badged for Sauber's primary sponsor – the Malaysian state petrochemical corporation, Petronas – and features several of its own unique evolutions, masterminded by former Ferrari engineer Osamu Goto.

Sauber has longer-term ambitions to develop its own engine. The team, based at Hinwil, achieved huge success in international sports-prototype racing before graduating to Formula 1 in 1993. The 1998-model Sauber C17 was designed by Leo Ress.

In 1997, Sauber conducted a novel 'back-to-back' test by requesting Michael Schumacher to drive its car at Ferrari's Fiorano proving track and offer his feedback on how the Swiss chassis compared with its Italian counterpart. Everybody concerned stayed tight-lipped about Schumacher's conclusions, but it was rumoured that the German World Champion felt Sauber's chassis was superior to Ferrari's...

There are limitations, strictly enforced by the FIA, on the types of materials which can be employed in the construction of a Formula 1 engine. *Some* exotic materials – most of which originated in the aerospace industry and tend to be extremely expensive – are incorporated in Formula 1 engines, but others are banned. For example, carbon and aramid fibre-reinforced materials cannot be used for the pistons, cylinder heads and block, and only ferrous metals may be used for the crankshaft and cams.

Exotic materials can offer advantages from the weight-saving standpoint, but the FIA wishes to curb excesses in 'unhelpful' expenditure – taking the view that if one manufacturer made widespread use of such materials, the others would rapidly follow suit, so there would be no particular benefit to anyone.

Ceramic materials offer certain advantages for areas of the engine which get very hot, but although some Formula 1 engines do contain a few ceramic components, the theoretical benefits are often outweighed by drawbacks. The beneficial properties of ceramics include their resistance to temperature-induced expansion and contraction: in fact, their dimensions hardly fluctuate at all. While that makes them capable of maintaining close tolerances at very high temperatures, they are difficult to actually incorporate alongside metal components – because the very fact that their expansion and contraction characteristics *are* so different makes them incompatible.

Carbons and other composite materials often present a similar dilemma: they are theoretically better, but in reality there are enormous difficulties involved in using them in engines, particularly in fixing them to metal components.

Some advanced materials – such as metal matrix composites (MMCs), which are metals mixed with non-metallic elements such as carbon fibres – go some way towards achieving the best of both worlds, because they offer a *combination* of properties. The little pieces of fibre in the metal help to reinforce the construction, or can add strength in a particular direction, allowing less material to be used and thereby saving weight.

The extent to which exotic materials are incorporated into Formula 1 engines must be put into perspective. Typically, almost two-thirds of the components are made of aluminium, while almost one-third are made of steel. Only approximately five per cent of the components are made from other materials – and those materials include titanium, magnesium and carbonfibre, which can hardly be considered 'exotic' by the standards of MMCs and suchlike – so the proportion of new-breed materials is actually very small. The most significant single contributor to engine materials technology over the past five years has been the improvement in such manufacturing techniques as casting and surface-coating.

Renault officially departed Formula 1 at the end of the 1997 Grand Prix season, after a dazzling run of successes. Its engine has lived on, however – being supplied to the Williams and Benetton teams by one of Renault's major technical partners, Mecachrome.

The engines are being supplied on a wholly commercial basis to Williams and Benetton, who have to pay for any development they want done. The price of a supply of Mecachrome-Renault engines for one year is said to be a cool £12.5 million. Williams will use the Mecachrome engine for two seasons to fill the gap before its new engine partner, BMW – which departed Formula 1 at the end of 1987 – returns in 2000. Benetton has badged the Mecachrome engine with one of its brands, Playlife.

Renault's swansong year in Formula 1 was a fairytale one, as – in partnership with Williams – it clinched its eleventh World title from the twelve available in the six years since it re-entered motorsport's premier category (only Michael Schumacher's 1994 World Drivers' title with Benetton-Ford denied Renault a clean sweep). Renault also equalled Honda's record of six consecutive World Constructors' titles.

The Mecachrome-Renault engine, designed under the inspired leadership of Bernard Dudot, has a 71-degree cylinder bank angle. The vee angle is a fundamental factor in the overall balancing of an engine, allowing some of the major out-of-balance forces to be cancelled out. The vee angle is also a significant factor in the packaging of the engine within the car. A wider engine, for example, can actually contribute to the overall stiffness of the car – although there will then be a negative effect in other ways. Since the days of the legendary Ford-Cosworth DFV, which had a vee angle of 90 degrees, engines have tended to get narrower. The minimum angle in recent years has been 65 degrees, but the norm today is 70-75 degrees.

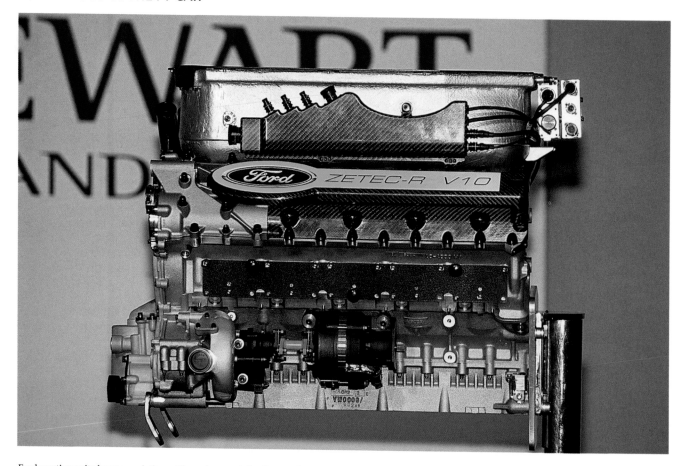

Ford continues its long association with engine specialist Cosworth to supply the Stewart team free of charge as a full 'works' entry, and two other teams – Tyrrell and Minardi – as paying customers, both reputed to be paying US$7.5 million for their supply in 1998.

For the 1998 season, an all-new V10 Ford-Cosworth Zetec-R engine emerged. Stewart gets this new unit exclusively, while the 'customer teams' get the older engine – prepared by a totally separate operation within the Cosworth organisation so as to maintain confidentiality for the Stewart team – to which they contribute their own development efforts.

All Formula 1 engines have double over-head camshaft (DOHC) systems, and pneumatic valve actuation. First adopted by Renault in the quest for higher revs, pneumatic valve control – in which compressed air is used to operate the valves, instead of potentially fragile springs – is now universal in Formula 1.

On its works engines, Ford has abandoned the chain-drive timing system which was the cause of much unreliability in 1997, in favour of the more popular option: gear-driven camshafts. The engines supplied to the two customer teams retained the chain-drive system, but incorporated modifications intended to make it more dependable.

The poor engine reliability suffered by the Stewart team marred an otherwise promising debut season. The team had a particularly torrid time at the British Grand Prix, when Ford adopted a high-risk approach to their development programme by running unproven evolutions of their engine in the full glare of global publicity – and had no fewer than five units fail in qualifying and the race.

The Japanese Mugen concern, an offshoot of the giant Honda organisation, supplies the Jordan team with a potent powerplant which is the envy of many teams. An entirely new Mugen-Honda engine was fielded for 1998 – an indication of the seriousness of the Japanese manufacturer's intentions.

Could Mugen's involvement be the stalking horse for a full-blooded campaign by Honda in 2000? Many pundits think so, and that is certainly causing concerns for the other engine manufacturers in Formula 1. No-one has forgotten that, during nine years with first Williams and then McLaren, Honda won five World Drivers' titles, a record six consecutive World Constructors' titles (from 1986 to 1991 inclusive), and 69 Grands Prix.

The new Mugen-Honda V10 is smaller, lighter and lower than its predecessor, which was based on the company's earlier 3.5-litre unit. The drive to make engines smaller is motivated by the desire to make more room for the rear diffuser and other aerodynamic devices, and also to help lower the car's centre of gravity.

Jordan's contract with Mugen-Honda ensures its supply throughout 1998 and 1999.

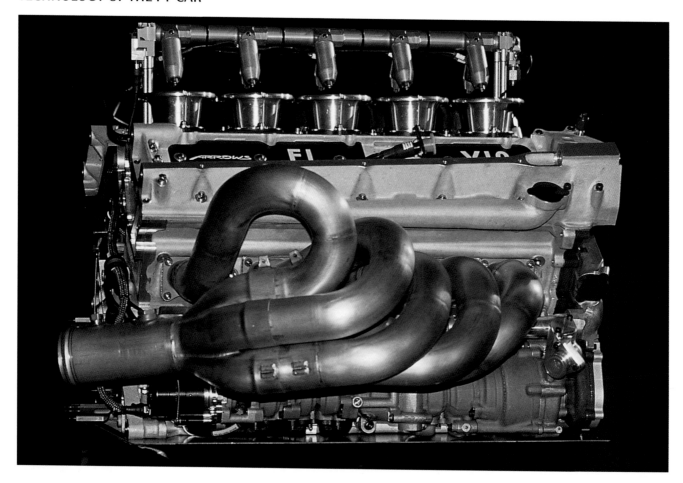

The introduction of new chassis regulations in 1998 has inevitably had an impact on engine packaging. Those engine manufacturers which introduced all-new engines for that year, such as Ford-Cosworth and Mugen-Honda, had the advantage of being able to tailor their units better than the other engine manufacturers, who could only make such changes as their existing units allowed.

Formula 1's all-new engines are significantly different from their predecessors from the installation stand-point, because the requirement for a narrower rear track had a major effect on the aerodynamics – reducing the space available for the rear diffuser and the flow of hot air from the radiators, and thereby eroding down-force and cooling capabilities, which had then to be clawed back as much as possible.

This is the all-new engine used exclusively by the Arrows team, which has commissioned independent engine-builder Brian Hart to head its own 'in-house' engine department – putting Arrows in Ferrari's league! Arrows's previous engine supplier was Yamaha, which withdrew from Formula 1 at the end of 1997 after failing to win a single Grand Prix. The Yamaha engine was developed in partnership with tuning specialist John Judd's Engine Developments concern.

Arrows is based at Leafield, near Witney, and enjoys the ambitious leadership of Tom Walkinshaw. With the design skills of John Barnard and second-to-none facilities, much is now expected of the team, which – in twenty years of trying – has failed to win a single Grand Prix.

Among the most powerful engines in Formula 1 is the Peugeot unit. Peugeot patriotically supports the Prost equipe, having supplied first McLaren and then Jordan in previous seasons.

For throttle operation, Formula 1 cars have electronic 'fly-by-wire' systems in which there is no physical connection between the throttle pedal and the engine. The driver still depresses the pedal against a return spring in the time-honoured tradition, but instead of this activating a throttle cable, an electrical sensor (a potentiometer) in the pedal mechanism tells the car's electronic control system what the pedal's rotational position is, in response to which it activates the throttle actuators remotely – usually hydraulically.

The advantage this offers is that there no longer needs to be a uniform relationship between the driver's throttle pedal position and the position of the throttles themselves, so changes can be made to the throttle characteristics to suit the unique combination of the circuit conditions and the driver's personal preferences. These changes are made via the software, and can be undertaken at leisure prior to the race meeting, or during breaks in testing, practice or qualifying.

In 1997, Ferrari devised a method of programming the throttle system to automatically feather periodically as the car accelerated, and so achieve the smoothest possible torque curve throughout the rev range. This '3D throttle mapping' caused consternation among the other teams – although several then proceeded to field versions of their own.

Initially, the FIA tolerated these systems, provided they did not respond to wheelspin by reducing the revs – in which case they would have constituted a form of traction-control, outlawed at the end of 1993 as part of a general purge on technologies which diminished the driver's control. Every Formula 1 car is fitted with an engine data-logger – a black box which can be removed at random for a minute analysis of the software governing the engine's functioning – so at least the FIA could monitor the behaviour of the system Ferrari and others had so boldly introduced to ensure that the fine line into automatic traction-control was not being crossed.

For 1998, the FIA issued a 'clarification' concerning these systems which effectively outlawed them in their original form.

Entering a corner, the driver has lifted his foot off the throttle pedal. The engine is now on the 'over-run' – retarding the car rather than accelerating it – and the flames belching from its exhaust pipes are the result of unburnt combustion products being ignited by the intensely hot pipes.

The exhaust system plays a crucial role in the performance of the engine. It does much more than simply expel spent gases from the engine after each combustion cycle...

A single piston travelling within a ten-cylinder, 3-litre engine should theoretically draw in one-third of a litre of air on the induction stroke – but, *in fact*, a highly efficient Formula 1 engine draws in much more than that, despite the fact that turbocharging and supercharging are prohibited. By cramming more air in, a proportionate amount more fuel can also be squirted in – creating more power.

This 'quart into a pint pot' effect is a fundamental aspect of engine tuning. It is achieved by exploiting the pressure waves generated within the engine by the combustion cycle, ensuring that they arrive at just the right times to draw extra air in before the valves snap shut and the pistons pummel upwards. These pressure pulses travel at the speed of sound and are strongly influenced by the harmonics of the exhaust system. By carefully adjusting the lengths of the exhaust pipes, the harmonics can be altered – in much the same way that organ pipes create specific sound frequencies according to their lengths.

The distance from the valve down to the end of the tailpipe is critical to the exhaust pipe tuning. The complex 'spaghetti' of exhaust pipes seen sprouting from Formula 1 engines results from the need to achieve specific pipe lengths, whilst at the same time minimising the severity of performance-sapping bends by incorporating smoothly curving transitions from end to end – yet keeping the exhaust system tucked away as much as possible from the airflow passing on either side of the engine.

TECHNOLOGY OF THE F1 CAR

A critical factor in designing the exhaust system is its impact on the overall packaging in that region of the car. The exhaust pipes are situated immediately behind the radiators, and their presence there creates a 'blockage' effect, impeding the flow of air leaving the radiators and thereby compromising their cooling efficiency. The packaging is very tight in that region anyway, because the bodywork tapers in there, Coke bottle-style, around the rear wheels. So for the car designer, a complex series of trade-offs must be made – and, with the aerodynamic efficiency of the car taking first priority, as ever, the exhaust system must be as neat and compact as possible. This is another contributor to the current unpopularity of 12-cylinder engines: they have more exhaust pipes to be squeezed in.

Another constraint on the design of the exhaust system is the need for the tailpipes to protrude through the rear diffuser at the precise positions specified by the car aerodynamicists, following extensive windtunnel testing. The input of high-energy exhaust gases into this region, which is very sensitive aerodynamically, can have a critical influence on the car's stability.

Although the final shape of the exhaust system is decided by the car manufacturer, the length and diameter of the pipes are decided by the engine manufacturer. The car manufacturers make their own exhaust systems – usually from Inconel: a heat-resistant alloy originally developed for the aerospace industry and commonly used in aero-engines. On occasion, exhaust pipes are manufactured in one piece, rather than being fabricated from several segments.

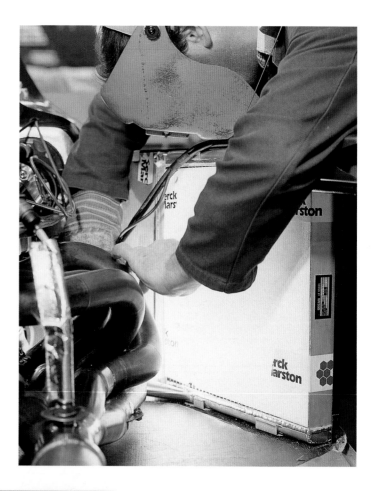

Installed in the outer ends of both exhaust manifolds are tiny sensors which continuously sample the oxygen content of the exhaust emissions. Known as Lambda sensors, they relay data directly to the engine management system, which adjusts the air-to-fuel ratio accordingly to ensure that the engine is always achieving complete combustion when the throttle is depressed.

Just as the distance from the valve down to the end of the tailpipe is critical to the exhaust pipe tuning, so the same principle applies to the air inlet ports. Here, the distance from the valve up to the inlet trumpet lip is the critical measurement for tuning.

All of the current Formula 1 engines have four valves per cylinder, and many have variable inlet trumpets. These allow the inlet tract to telescope in synchronisation with the engine revs, maintaining the optimum tuned length throughout the rev range. The *disadvantage* of variable trumpets is their operating mechanism, which adds weight to the top of the engine, raising its centre of gravity, and adds bulk which can compromise the car designer's efforts to have a low, neatly sculpted engine cover. The trumpets themselves are made of either aluminium – highly polished – or carbonfibre, while the lightweight structure which carries them, the trumpet tray, is made of carbonfibre.

The ambient air pressure and temperature have a significant influence on the engine's performance. In very hot weather, or at circuits situated well above sea level, the engine does not perform as well as it does at lower altitudes and temperatures.

Engine development is relentless. Manufacturers are constantly working to improve the airflow into the engine and the passage of gases through it to improve performance.

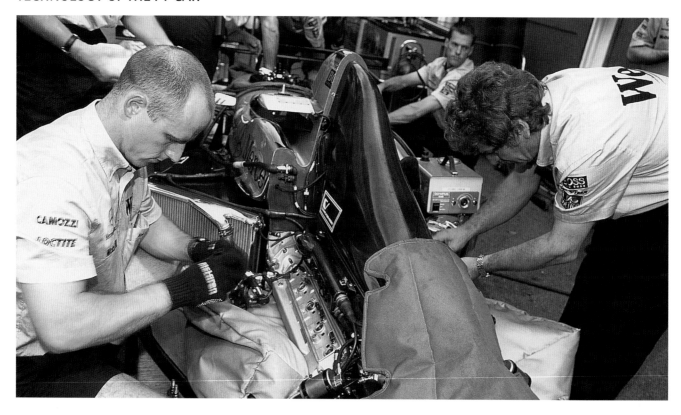

To attain its maximum performance, the engine must be able to induct the required volume of air efficiently. Great care is therefore necessary when determining the shape and size of the air inlet duct, or 'snorkel': the curved carbonfibre tube which channels air down from the streamlined aperture in the rollover hoop to the trumpet tray.

When the car is being designed, the engine's breathing needs – more formally termed the air mass flow requirement – must be fully catered for, and it is important to ensure not only that the correct volume of air will be delivered to the inlet ports, but also that it will be delivered as free from turbulence as possible, so all of the cylinders receive an equal supply.

Contrary to popular belief, the snorkel is not designed to ram air down into the engine, creating a form of supercharging. In fact, it does the *opposite*: it is actually designed to *slow down* the incoming air in order to create that effect more efficiently. It does this by progressively widening downstream of the frontal opening, causing the incoming air to slow down in the same way that the flow of water slows down when a river becomes wider. As the air slows down, its pressure goes up – effectively creating a form of forced induction into the engine.

The designer does not have an entirely free hand in determining the shape of the snorkel, because it must be fitted within the tight confines of the engine cover, the shape of which is critical to the overall aerodynamic efficiency of the car – and, in particular, to the efficient functioning of the rear aerofoil assemblies. It is also very important to ensure that the driver's helmet will not interfere with the flow of air into the snorkel: a couple of years ago, before proper attention was given to this problem, some drivers had to tilt their heads to one side on long straights to clear a path for the incoming air!

To perfect the design of the snorkel, windtunnel testing and computational fluid dynamics (CFD) studies are combined with actual engine tests on the dynamometer, using a powerful fan to flow air into the snorkel.

Cooling a Formula 1 engine is a major challenge. The size and shape of the radiators are refined during wind-tunnel testing, as they have a major influence on the aerodynamic performance of the car – due to their impeding effect on the airflow – as well as the performance of the engine.

The engine water and oil are cooled by means of radiators mounted at the aft end of carbonfibre ducts (radiator ducts) housed within both sidepods. Some cars have a symmetrical arrangement with 'split' water and oil radiators on either side. Others have an asymmetric arrangement with a water radiator only on one side and split water and oil radiators on the other. The radiator arrangement is generally dictated by the layout of the engine's oil scavenging system, but designers aim to have the minimum amount of pipework in order to save weight. As one put it, 'The *lightest* water pipe is not to have one!'

On the starting grid, engine cooling is maintained by installing fans in the entrances to the radiator ducts and the air inlet snorkel.

Designers are constantly striving to reduce the size of the radiators, in order to reduce the car's aerodynamic drag – and also to reduce the overall weight of the car, because less radiator volume translates into less water and oil being carried. The radiators have themselves become progressively lighter over recent years, thanks to improved construction techniques – particularly for the radiator core material.

Increasingly, Formula 1 engine manufacturers are designing their engines to 'run hotter' so that the size of the radiators can be reduced. They do this not only by improving the heat-rejection capabilities of the engine itself – by achieving a more efficient use of the flow of cooling water through the engine block and cylinder heads – but also by preventing excessive heat build-up from occurring in the first place, by designing the engine internals so that undue oil agitation is avoided.

This is certainly an attractive route to take, because although engines tend to produce less power the hotter they become, the aerodynamic advantages alone outweigh the slight loss of horsepower. However, diminishing the radiator size can pose a problem when a driver spins his car, because the sudden increase in temperature when air ceases to flow through the radiators poses a far higher risk of damage when engine cooling is already marginal.

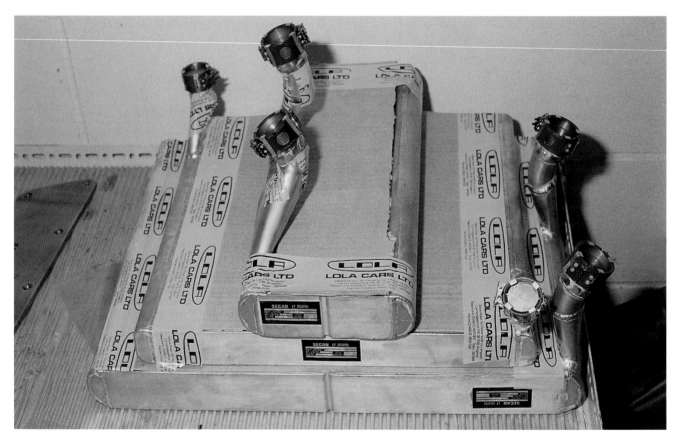

Although some engine manufacturers demand that their creations are lubricated with specially formulated oils, most are content with lubricants which the average motorist can buy off-the-shelf. In both cases, the oil is synthetic.

The same approach does not apply to the fuel, which – although it is essentially, by regulation, 'street standard' – is always specially concocted. In actual fact, there is very little performance-gain from the painstaking effort of special processing, but it *optimises* the fuel to provide the maximum performance within the limited scope allowed by the regulations.

All Formula 1 engines run on unleaded petroleum – by regulation – and they are all fuel-injected. Fuel consumption can be as high as 1.4 km to the litre (4 miles to the gallon). So during the Monaco Grand Prix – which covers 232 km (144 miles) – a car might consume as much as 166 litres (36 gallons) of fuel.

FIA inspectors police the fuel regulations very strictly, as this is an area where teams could readily gain an illegal advantage. The fuel must contain the same components used in roadgoing car fuels, and in similar concentrations – and must be pre-approved before the team can use it.

Employing advanced techniques such as gas chromatography and mass spectrometry, FIA inspectors measure the lead, sulphur, benzene, distillation and density of the fuel batch, accumulating a database of every component and its concentration in the fuel. This provides a unique 'footprint' of the fuel, which must be matched exactly when samples are subsequently taken at random during race meetings. The inspectors patrol the pitlane remorselessly, upholding the last letter of the law and threatening transgressors with Draconian penalties.

As part of its policing effort, the FIA has a custom-built articulated truck which carries all of the equipment needed to analyse fuel, as well as computer equipment to analyse software downloaded from the various on-car data recorders. This mobile laboratory is taken to every Grand Prix in Europe.

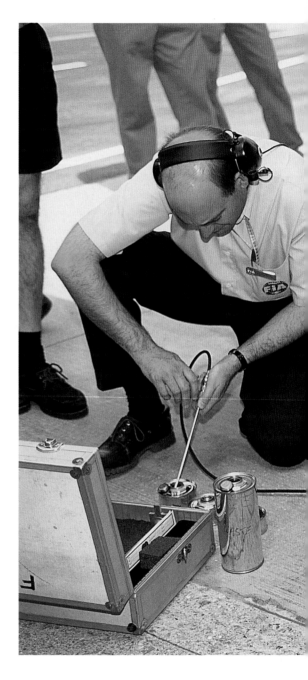

FIA regulations stipulate that the car's entire fuel load must be carried in an approved safety cell: a flexible rubber bladder, firmly anchored into the chassis to support it against the harsh manoeuvring of the car. It is designed to deform if it sustains a major impact, rather than rupturing with potentially disastrous consequences. The regulations state that no part of this cell may be ahead of the driver, so it is housed immediately behind the seat-back bulkhead.

The car designer's aim is to ensure that the made-to-measure cell occupies the smallest possible volumetric space within the chassis. When calculating the car's weight distribution, he must also take account of the changing weight of the fuel load during the course of a race. The shape of the fuel cell should be such that the fuel pick-up is constant, and not allow fuel to become stranded out of reach of the lift pumps. To ensure that the last remnants of fuel can be scavenged by the lift pumps – and to control the sloshing of the fuel under cornering, acceleration and braking loads – baffles and 'traps' are incorporated within the cell.

Some Formula 1 cars have two lift pumps, others three, strategically placed to achieve total fuel pick-up. The pumps deliver the fuel to a collector, housed within the cell, which provides a constant supply to another pump which feeds the engine – and is, in turn, driven by it. At the top of the fuel cell, mated to the chassis structure, is a magnesium or aluminium plate called the 'tank top'. This carries the air vent valve and the cell drain pipe valve, as well as the valves through which fuel is delivered to the engine and carried back via the return pipe. The latter valves incorporate a breakaway safety coupling which would prevent fuel flowing from the cell and posing a fire risk if the engine became detached from the chassis in a very major accident.

Fuel is loaded into the cell through an adaptor recessed into the side of the car, close to the cockpit. There are actually *two* adaptors – one on either side, because the circuits visited by the Formula 1 teams run in both clockwise and anticlockwise directions.

Teams took to covering the redundant adaptor with a lightweight fairing to improve streamlining, but as a result of a new regulation introduced for 1998, each adaptor is now protected by a hinged carbonfibre cover strong enough to withstand opening in an accident. These covers must be locked in place whenever the car is on the racetrack.

Since its introduction in 1994, refuelling has been a source of controversy – with fears expressed for the safety of drivers and pitlane personnel alike. A fuel-fed fire in a congested pitlane could indeed cause injuries on a significant scale, so safety is taken very seriously. Pit crew members actually responsible for refuelling the cars wear comprehensive protection against fire penetration and smoke inhalation, and rehearse constantly to perfect their skills.

The pitlane refuelling rigs are manufactured under exclusive licence by Intertechnique, a company with a strong aerospace background. They are pressurised and have a capacity of 200 litres (44 gallons).

Refuelling has added a whole new dimension to race strategy. Teams must decide whether to undertake one, two or even three pit-stops – and when. The refuelling strategy affects not only the time spent driving into and out of the pitlane and actually taking the fuel on board, but also the lap times of the cars: team strategists are mindful of the fact that every 10 kg (22 lb) of fuel carried adds half-a-second to the lap time.

Following the introduction of race refuelling, the single most significant impact on the design of the cars is that they have become smaller, as they no longer need to carry a large enough fuel load to complete the full race distance.

The siting of engine ancillaries and electrical black boxes is partly governed by weight-distribution considerations, but mainly by the availability of space within the cramped confines of the car's interior. For example, on some cars the alternator is placed in the vee between the cylinder banks, where it might have to vie for space with assorted elements of the water, fuel and hydraulic systems – and also, in some cases, the throttle actuators and variable-trumpet actuators.

Ancillaries and black boxes can also be squeezed into the narrow space between the top of the chassis and the engine air inlet snorkel, in the narrow gaps between the outer surfaces of the radiator ducts and the inner surfaces of the sidepods, in gaps between the outer surfaces of the chassis and the inner surfaces of the radiator ducts, and even inside the cockpit. Black boxes are installed on rubber mountings to insulate them from excessive vibration.

A Formula 1 car typically has over a mile of cabling installed within it. The routing of wires must be such that there is sufficient clearance to avoid chafing.

Every Formula 1 engine is tested on a dynamometer after being completely rebuilt between uses. A rebuild takes approximately 200 hours.

Typically, the engine first undergoes a very carefully controlled running-in period on the 'dyno', after which it is put through a setting-up procedure which optimises the delivery of fuel into the cylinders, and the ignition, for that particular unit. A power-curve test is then undertaken, to ensure that it runs properly all the way up to maximum speed. The engine is then removed from the dyno and undergoes the best part of a day of further checks to make sure that any fault which may have arisen during running, but escaped detection, is duly discovered and rectified.

It is then crated up and delivered to the team, where it ideally has a 400-km (250-mile) 'life' before being rebuilt once more – although some engines are run for up to 650 km (400 miles) before being returned for rebuild.

As well as testing rebuilt engines, dynamometers are used in the relentless drive to develop modifications which give better engine performance. Engines are also tested on 'transient' dynamometers. These are equipped to accurately simulate actual race conditions, rather than testing engines in a sterile laboratory environment.

Formula 1 clutches – which are supplied to the teams by two manufacturers, AP Racing and Sachs – are electro-hydraulically activated. Due to the phenomenal revving capability of Formula 1 engines, clutch plates rotate at speeds as high as 17,500 rpm and are subjected to temperatures as high as 500 degrees C when the driver slips the clutch on the starting grid.

The clutch operates as part of the semi-automatic gearshifting system. On upshifts, the system does not usually activate the clutch at all – it merely drops the engine revs momentarily – but it must declutch for downshifts.

Like many other components in Formula 1, clutches have become ever smaller and lighter. A typical unit weighs just 1.5 kg (3.3 lb), and has a maximum external diameter of less than 140 mm (5.5 in). It has seven carbon plates, 115 mm (4.5 in) in diameter: four intermediate plates and three drive plates.

The driver brings the engine revs up to 11,000–12,000 rpm for the start. Perhaps surprisingly, the parts of the clutch most vulnerable to overheating are not the plates themselves, but the housings which hold them – which are made of titanium – and the diaphragm spring, which is made of steel.

All Formula 1 cars have semi-automatic gearboxes, operated with fingertip precision – via either high-pressure hydraulics or pneumatics – by two paddles mounted immediately behind the steering wheel. Some cars have a six-speed gearbox, others seven-speed.

A single reverse gear is a mandatory requirement, and the capability to reverse must be demonstrated during scrutineering. Furthermore, the cars must have a drive-disengagement system, so they can be removed more easily if they are abandoned at the trackside: this is activated by a button in the cockpit, the location of which is denoted externally on some cars by an *N* (for 'Neutral') symbol.

Transverse gearboxes are used in Formula 1, but the vast majority of designers opt for a longitudinal arrangement. The latter re-emerged after several years out of favour when the FIA imposed severe restrictions on the length of the rear diffuser in 1994. A longitudinal layout lends itself more readily to incorporation in a narrow gearbox casing, thereby allowing extra space to be gifted back to the rear diffuser. Unlike earlier-generation longitudinal gearboxes, today's versions have the gears clustered *ahead* of the rear axle line, where their mass – within the wheelbase – improves the car's weight distribution.

With up to 12 steel or titanium studs, the gearbox is joined to the engine via an intermediary structure known as the bellhousing, which houses the clutch and the engine oil tank on most cars, although the 1998-model Stewart SF-2 has its oil tank set in a tall, narrow recess in the back of the chassis in order to bring weight forward and reduce the pipework. On most cars, the bellhousing is integral with the gearbox, but on some it is a separate unit.

Weight is a particularly critical factor in the design of the gearbox – because it is sited so far back, and therefore exerts much more influence on the weight distribution and general handling of the car. In an effort to make the gearbox as light as possible, a designer can be tempted to reduce the casing wall thickness – but if he reduces it too much, major problems will arise when the car has to run. The gearbox will not be rigid enough to prevent it from flexing under the structural loads fed in from the rear suspension and rear aerofoil assemblies, which are mounted directly onto it.

Such flexing would, at the very least, adversely affect the car's handling. It would also degrade the efficiency of the gear ratios within – which run to minute tolerances – and, at worst, cause the gearbox to seize completely.

TECHNOLOGY OF THE F1 CAR

The evolution of gearbox construction in Formula 1 has been just as dramatic as the evolution of chassis structures and engine components. Some years ago, cast gearbox casings gave way to fabricated casings in the drive to reduce manufacturing lead-times and increase stiffness and lightness. Casting of gearbox casings, usually from magnesium, consumes time because of the need to fashion complex patterns from which the casings can be cast.

Fabrication of gearbox casings – pioneered in 1994 by Ferrari designer John Barnard, who also introduced the first carbonfibre bellhousing the following year – circumvented this process. But then the quest for increased performance led some teams to develop even more lightweight, stiffer casings made from carbonfibre locally reinforced by titanium plates and fittings – in spite of the fact that carbonfibre construction also requires pattern-making.

The latest gearbox manufacturing method – an all-carbonfibre construction deployed by the Stewart and Arrows teams at the start of the 1998 season – is indeed a radical evolution: graphic evidence, if ever it were needed, that the search for higher performance is unending.

In taking such an ambitous step, Stewart and Arrows were intent on introducing even greater stiffness, lightness and compactness into the gearbox casing. The other Formula 1 teams – several of which had experimented with carbonfibre gearbox casings – had shied away from actually racing them, due to doubts about their reliability: the forces acting on a gearbox are much more difficult to predict than those acting on the other carbonfibre structures, such as the aerofoil assemblies or the chassis itself.

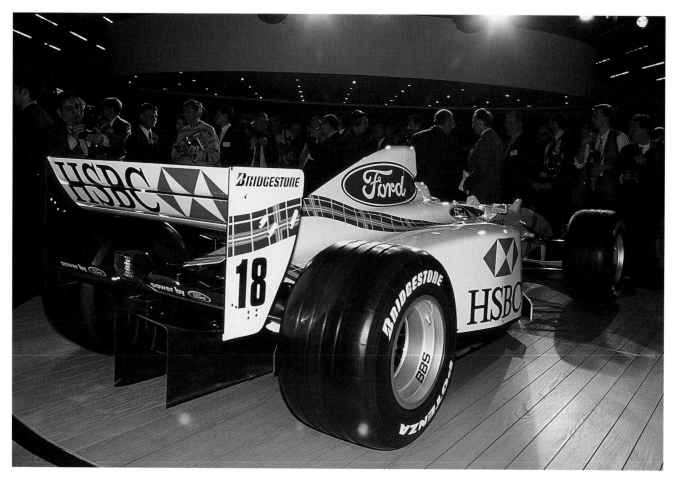

The gearbox oil must be capable of performing well in an exceptionally punishing environment. Gearbox oil temperatures can reach around 125 degrees C, and the pressures between the gear teeth are phenomenal. At any given moment in time, virtually the entire motive power of the engine is being transmitted through a fingerprint-sized area of gear tooth surface – and, theoretically at least, metal never touches metal: contact is limited to the oil film.

Gearbox oil cooling is accomplished by either routing the gearbox oil through the engine oil cooling system or mounting a small, dedicated radiator at the rear of the car.

Following a trend set by Benetton in 1994, most Formula 1 cars are fitted with hydraulically actuated, electronically controlled differentials. These incorporate load-measuring sensors which constantly measure the torque generated by the driveshafts and make adjustments to the drive according to a pre-programmed regime.

There was some concern that the introduction of electronic differentials would provide a back-door route to automatic traction control, but they were allowed to stay under the sweeping new regulations introduced for 1998, provided they mimic the behaviour of a known mechanical differential. Also, settings can only be changed in the pits, not whilst the car is in motion.

Continuously variable transmissions (CVTs), which allow the engine to maintain peak efficiency at virtually all times, were banned by the FIA after the Williams team began experimenting with such systems in 1993: David Coulthard actually tested a CVT-equipped Williams at Silverstone on one occasion. It is said that the ban was introduced because spectators would find the sound of an entire grid of cars running at full throttle for virtually the whole race monotonous!

The driveshafts, and the constant-velocity joints at their extremities, cope with enormous forces and have evolved considerably over recent years. They have become lighter and more compact as a result of improvements in both materials and design, and a steady shift away from the use of proprietary parts to purpose-made components. In 1997, Williams – uniquely – angled their driveshafts backwards, by ten degrees, to allow the gearbox to be sited further forward for improved weight distribution. Stewart followed suit in 1998, moving the gearbox forward by about 25 mm (1 in).

chapter **5** BRAKES

BRAKES are a key contributor to the extraordinary performance of Formula 1 cars. The task of reining in the kinetic energy of a hurtling racing car is nothing short of Herculean. The cars can accelerate from rest to 160 kph (100 mph) and decelerate back to a standstill again in a fraction over six seconds. In short, the accelerative prowess of the engine is more than matched by the decelerative muscle of the brakes.

Formula 1 drivers leave their braking seemingly impossibly late. Their cars can decelerate from 320 kph (200 mph) on a long straight to 80 kph (50 mph) for a slow corner in just 100 metres (330 feet) and three seconds. When achieving such phenomenal performance levels, friction between the discs and pads generates temperatures as high as 750 degrees C. The brakes smoulder dull red, then glow bright yellow with the effort.

Prior to the introduction of grip-reducing regulations for 1998, deceleration forces under braking at high-speed circuits such as Hockenheim and Monza peaked at almost 6 G. Now, the maximum value is around 4 G – but greater performance will come in time, when development reaches full maturity.

When the calipers grasp the discs, the strain on all of the components is immense. Modern Formula 1 cars have carbon-carbon brake discs, which are more durable than the cast-iron discs they had in the past. To perform at their full potential, carbon discs must be brought up to a very high operating temperature. If they exceed this they become less efficient, so to help maintain them within the desired temperature band the discs are ventilated by ram-air directed at strategic points by carbonfibre ducts.

An overheating disc can disintegrate in spectacular fashion – as Williams driver Heinz-Harald Frentzen found when his left-front disc literally exploded during the 1997 Australian Grand Prix, costing him a podium place. Nevertheless, among the sweeping series of rule-changes introduced for 1998 were restrictions on the size and positioning of the cooling ducts for the rear brakes, which must now match those for the front. Also introduced was a restriction on the thickness of the brake discs, which had previously been unlimited. The new limit is 28 mm (1.1 in).

This was an effort by the FIA to limit braking performance, by forcing manufacturers to limit the friction between the discs and pads in order to last the race distance.

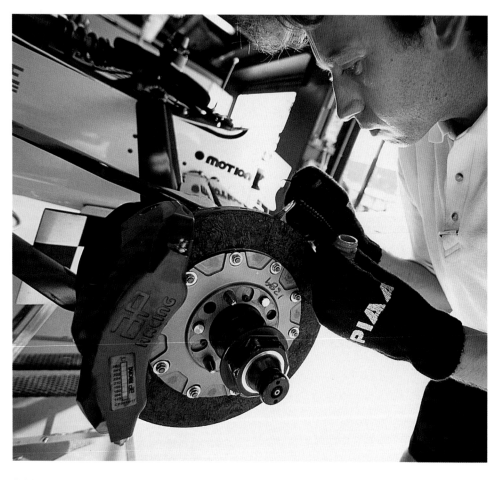

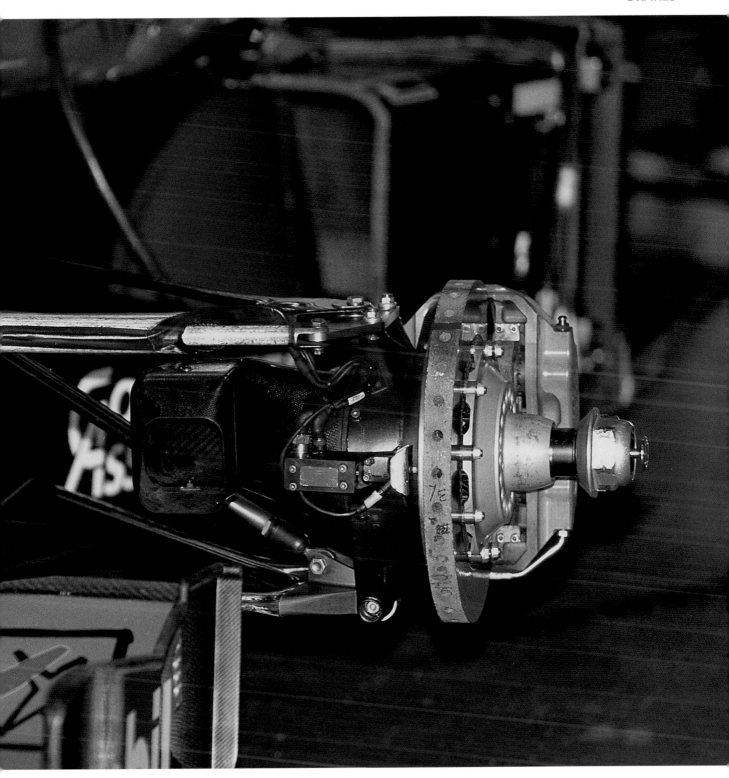

Like the brake discs, Formula 1 brake pads are made from carbon-carbon.

Most Formula 1 cars have six-piston brake calipers at both front and rear, but some have four-pot calipers at the rear. The calipers are made purely from aluminium. Until recently, it was possible to create metal-matrix composite (MMC) calipers by mixing in other materials – such as silicon carbide particles – to stiffen, strengthen and lighten the end product. These exotic additives have been outlawed for 1998 in an effort to contain cost and performance.

By regulation, Formula 1 cars have two separate brake circuits (operated by the same pedal) to ensure that if one circuit fails the other will still act on at least two of the wheels. Drivers can adjust the brake balance between the front and rear wheels, to help avoid locking one pair under heavy braking: under normal conditions, a little under 60 per cent bias is placed on the front brakes, but for wet-weather running most of the braking bias is transferred to the rear.

Anti-lock braking systems have been outlawed since 1993.

During the 1997 season, several teams – led by Williams – introduced electronic brake-balance systems, activated by buttons on the steering wheel and driven by two electronically controlled hydraulic pumps. These were pre-programmed for each corner and offered a far greater degree of precision over the previous manual (cable-operated) systems, because they allowed the driver to revert to the previous setting *exactly* if he so wished.

Electronic brake-balance systems were initially permitted – provided they were programmed to behave in the same manner on each lap – on the grounds that they were driver-operated and did not actually *prevent* the wheels from locking (the software was inspectable). The systems typically incorporated sensors for measuring lateral and longitudinal G-forces, individual brake pressures, wheel speeds and brake disc temperatures, and foot pedal positions and pressures – and could even be programmed to operate on each wheel individually, rather than on the front and rear wheels as pairs.

They were outlawed for 1998, as part of the FIA's campaign to rid Formula 1 of what was widely perceived as a new wave of electronic aids which could diminish the drivers' display of virtuosity.

Left-foot braking has become popular in Formula 1, after being common practice in rallying for many years. A simple two-pedal arrangement offers the driver a notable advantage by removing the fractional time-lapse between lifting his foot off the accelerator pedal and locating it on the brake pedal. The clutch activator is operated by hand, being located immediately behind the steering wheel.

One disadvantage is that, if the driver is unfortunate enough to get into a spin, with no clutch pedal to depress with his foot and his hands flailing around on the steering wheel, he is unlikely to be able to activate the hand-operated clutch in time to prevent the engine from stalling. The solution is to have a clutch pedal *as well*, thereby getting the best of both worlds.

During pitstops, the driver helps his pit crew by keeping his foot on the brake pedal.

A thick black cloud of carbon dust billows out from the brake units when the wheels are pulled clear, but the pit crew have protective masks over their mouths and noses, and goggles shielding their eyes.

Braking systems offer much potential for innovation and evolution – *if* the regulations permit it. Automatic traction-control is banned, but in the latter stages of the 1997 season McLaren fielded an ingenious braking system to aid traction out of slower corners. They fitted a second brake pedal to the left of the 'main' pedal. It only worked on the rear wheels and could be used by the driver to limit wheelspin. The extra brake pedal could be switched to retard either wheel individually, or to act on both wheels as a pair.

The system was kept a closely guarded secret, until observers noticed that the rear brake discs were glowing while the car was accelerating out of corners!

The idea was not entirely new. Williams and Minardi developed similar systems in the days when electronic driver aids were rife in Formula 1, but these were outlawed for 1994. McLaren's system was deemed legal on the grounds that it was driver-operated and therefore did not constitute an automatic traction-control function, but there were concerns that this type of technology could diminish the spectacle of Grand Prix racing.

Increasingly in Formula 1, the written regulations are 'fleshed out' by clarifications from the FIA in response to specific proposals from car designers: teams are obliged to ask when they wish to stray into a grey area. The FIA feels that governing in this manner is the only realistic way because designers will always find a route around published rules. McLaren's novel braking system – having been approved by one such clarification – has since been widely copied.

chapter 6 SUSPENSION, WHEELS & TYRES

TYRES became the focus of renewed attention when refuelling pitstops were reintro-
duced into Formula 1 in 1994. Television images of pit crews changing tyres with
amazing speed and precision when cars came in to refuel sparked the public imagina-
tion and highlighted the fact that Formula 1 is a *team* sport.

Very highly developed tyres, in concert with highly evolved aerodynamic devices, are the
key contributors to the phenomenal cornering performance of modern Formula 1 cars: lateral forces of over 3.5 G can be experienced through high-speed corners. Formula 1 tyres
have a maximum permissible width of 381 mm (15 in) – as they have had since the start of
the 1993 season – and, in a new regulation introduced for 1998, a *minimum* permissible
width of 305 mm (12 in) at the front and 356 mm (14 in) at the rear. They are of radial ply
construction and are tubeless.

Like the brake pads and discs, the tyres only operate at full efficiency when they have
reached the correct working temperature: normally around 125 degrees C at the tread. The
tyres are wrapped in electrically heated blankets to bring them closer to their optimum
temperature prior to the car being driven.

Formula 1 tyres are equipped with valve cores which differ from those used in roadgoing
car tyres in having seals capable of withstanding the much higher temperatures generated
in racing conditions. Operating pressures are lower than those of most roadgoing car tyres,
and varying the tyre pressures is one of the methods used to alter the handling of the car.

To minimise variables in the set-up, the quality of the air in the tyres is carefully controlled. The air is processed through special equipment linked to the compressors which
inflate the tyres, which converts it into a nitrogen-rich, moisture-free gas. This ensures that
each tyre retains constant inflation properties regardless of where it was inflated, and that
pressure variations due to changes in temperature are uniform. The high temperature build-
up in racing conditions can result in a pressure increase of as much as 10 psi. For this reason, the pressures are always measured and set when the tyres are at the optimum
operating temperature.

The 'weight' on a tyre due to the combined effects of the weight of the car, aerodynamic forces and cornering, braking and acceleration forces is known as the tyre loading. When a car is cornering, the loading on the outside tyres increases and the loading on the inside tyres decreases as the car's weight shifts laterally. The stiffness of the sidewall construction is a very important factor in the tyre's cornering performance, because this directly influences its responsiveness to the driver's steering inputs.

Weight distribution also has an important influence on the performance of the tyres. The car's heaviest components are unavoidably concentrated at the rear, placing a proportionately greater burden on the rear tyres. The rear tyres are, in any case, more heavily worked – because, while the front tyres only have to cope with cornering and braking forces, the rear tyres must generate tractive effort as well.

The G-forces acting on the tread are massive when the tyre is revolving at around 2800 rpm at top speed.

Along with the tread pattern, the constitution of the tread – the compound – plays a crucial role in determining the level of grip (adhesion) the tyre will generate, and also plays an important part in determining the tyre's wear characteristics. The four basic ingredients are rubber polymers, carbon blacks, oils and curatives.

Although the grip itself is generated at the contact patches between the tyres and the racetrack surface, the driver senses the level of grip through his hands and feet – and the seat of his pants!

Until recently, Goodyear was the only company which chose to supply Formula 1 tyres. Akron, Ohio-based Goodyear offered a range of tyres which suited the different types of circuits, compatible with all of the cars on the grid, and the situation was relatively straightforward. About 1500 tyres were sufficient for each event.

But then came competition and new regulations. Goodyear, the long-term campaigner, stated publicly that it welcomed the challenge from Japanese manufacturer Bridgestone, which entered Formula 1 at the start of the 1997 season. Almost half of the teams – but none of the top teams – signed up to use Bridgestone tyres. Development was stepped up and the battle for supremacy was on.

Instead of supplying just one dry-weather specification tyre at each race, as in previous years, new regulations introduced by the FIA for 1997 called for two different types to be supplied: 'prime' and 'optional' (the latter is generally a softer compound). The teams can run both of these tyre types during free practice, but have then to choose which type each car will qualify and race on. They must run one or the other; they are not permitted to mix tyre types by fitting a car with, say, prime-compound tyres on the front wheels and optional-compound tyres on the rear.

This new ruling, along with the need to offer a greater variety of wet-weather tyres – the result of competition from Bridgestone – meant that the number of tyres taken to each race increased dramatically. During 1997, about 2300 tyres were taken to each race by Goodyear alone – despite the fact that the American company was supplying far fewer teams than the year before.

To make matters even more difficult, new varieties of tyre had to be produced with ever-greater haste as the two tyre companies fought to gain an advantage. The 'tyre war' which raged between them through 1997 caused lap times to fall by as much as four seconds. During the course of that season, Goodyear was forced to build in excess of 30,000 tyres, of 61 different dry-weather specifications and 22 different wet-weather specifications. Comparing this to the previous year's tally of ten dry-weather specifications and eight wet-weather specifications gives some indication of how fierce the battle became.

Over the winter of 1997/8, McLaren and Benetton defected from Goodyear and gave Bridgestone strength in depth. This followed the American manufacturer's announcement that it would withdraw from Formula 1 at the end of 1998 – despite the fact that it had won on every occasion in 1997. Bridgestone finally scored its first Grand Prix victory at the first Grand Prix of 1998, at Melbourne in Australia, with Mika Häkkinen at the wheel of a McLaren.

The major change in the regulations for the start of the 1998 season, as the FIA strove to reduce cornering speeds in the interests of safety, stipulated that the cars had to be 20 cm (7.88 in) – ten per cent – narrower than before: the maximum permissible track was reduced from 200 cm (78.8 in) to 180 cm (70.92 in). The teams responded by moving the wheels closer to the car, by shortening the suspension, rather than reducing the body width of the car itself, as that would have reduced downforce.

Furthermore, the FIA required the cars to be fitted with grooved dry-weather tyres, instead of the slicks (bald-treaded tyres) used since 1970. There had to be three grooves in the front tyres and four grooves in the rear tyres – all 14 mm (0.55 in) wide tapering to 10 mm (0.39 in), 2.5 mm (0.09 in) deep and separated by 50 mm (1.97 in). This resulted in 17 per cent less rubber contact with the racetrack surface.

The influence of these new regulations on the performance of the cars was profound, but the ingenuity of the designers has subsequently disguised this fact. Ironically, the cars would be slightly *faster* on long straights, due to the reduction in aerodynamic drag resulting from their smaller frontal area. But, denied a proportion of rear diffuser width and precious rubber contact with the racetrack surface, they would be inherently slower into, through and out of corners, and slower away from the start line.

It was hoped that reduced grip levels might improve the quality of the racing – partly by increasing braking distances and thereby creating a larger 'overtaking zone'. Only time would tell.

The dry-weather grooved tyre is in a class of its own – neither a direct modification of the outlawed slick nor an adaptation of the wet-weather tyre; its introduction required a fundamentally different design philosophy. New compounds had to be developed, capable of performing to the maximum whilst having good wear characteristics. New constructions and materials were tested, and a wide range of new mould shapes were evolved by both manufacturers in an effort to create the best possible product.

Early testing with the new-specification, narrower cars with grooved tyres suggested that as much as six seconds had been added to lap times, but most of this deficit was won back as the teams and tyre manufacturers undertook intensive development work throughout the winter months. Perhaps surprisingly, braking distances increased only slightly, and although the cars had a tendency to slide more, the drivers modified their driving styles to account for this.

By the time the first Grand Prix of 1998 took place, the reduction in lap speeds was negligible – but at least the FIA could take credit for having kept the performance of the cars in check, for lap speeds would undoubtedly have been faster than the previous year if nothing had been done.

There were other changes to the tyre regulations for 1998. The number of tyres that may be used by each driver increased by four, to 40 for each event. The number of wet-weather tyres permitted per driver, per event remained the same at 28. However, the number of specifications of wet-weather tyre permitted to be used is no longer unlimited: now, manufacturers can supply only three specifications of wet-weather tyre at each event.

Wet-weather tyres can only be used when the racetrack has been declared officially 'wet' by the Race Director. Although they have a similar construction to dry-weather tyres, their tread pattern is very different. The grooves in the tread are designed to disperse as much water as possible, allowing the tread to grip the racetrack surface.

FIA regulations demand that the 'land/sea' ratio of a wet-weather tyre must be 75 per cent: 'land' refers to the tread surface and 'sea' refers to the grooves, meaning that 25 per cent of the total tread area has to be composed of grooves.

The aim when designing a wet-weather tyre is to ensure that it will operate efficiently across a wide spectrum of conditions, ranging from a damp to a partially flooded racetrack. The tyre must therefore be capable not only of removing whatever water is encountered, but also of maintaining its temperature so as to sustain optimum performance from the tyre compound. The tread pattern is crucial in this respect.

Overheating can cause a tyre to deteriorate rapidly, and wet-weather tyres are particularly susceptible to this if the track surface dries out too much. In order to prevent their wet-weather tyres from overheating, drivers often seek out a 'wet' racing line on a drying circuit by avoiding the 'tram lines' which emerge when cars have cleared standing water or moisture from the conventional racing line.

The two tyre manufacturers must transport to each Grand Prix all of the equipment necessary to fit the tyres to the wheels, inflate them, balance and demount them. They also bring computer equipment which undertakes stock control and relays engineering data to the main computers at their respective headquarters for further analysis.

Tyre technicians assigned to each team by the tyre manufacturers are kept busy throughout a Grand Prix meeting. One ongoing task is to monitor the state of the tyres every time a driver comes into the pits. The temperature and wear information they record provides a vital guide to the performance not only of the tyres, but also of the chassis and suspension. This data may also identify a change in the characteristics of the circuit, which may have undergone resurfacing work since the last time it was visited by Formula 1 cars.

An important factor in winning races is conserving the tyres. The driver's actions, or the racetrack conditions – or a combination of both – can cause sufficient damage to the surface of a tyre to severely degrade its performance. Common problems are graining, which is a 'tearing' of the tread surface generally caused by excessive lateral grip, and blistering, which is caused by overheating of the tread compound. Locking up a tyre by applying the brakes too hard – as seen here – can also severely degrade its performance. Three-times World Drivers' Champion Niki Lauda, now an advisor to the Ferrari team, once described this as 'the rape of a tyre'.

Inevitably, compromises must be made in the design of a racing tyre. For example, it must be as light as possible, in order to reduce unsprung weight and maximise road-holding, yet it has to be strong enough to withstand the enormous forces imposed on it. It has to offer as much grip as possible, yet it must have durability and offer consistent performance.

When a new tyre is put on a car it is referred to as a 'sticker' tyre, because it still bears the manufacturer's distinctive adhesive identification label. When it is used for the first time and brought up to operating temperature, it has undergone one heat cycle and is then described as 'scrubbed'.

The forged magnesium alloy wheels are supplied to the teams by proprietary manufacturers, including OZ, BBS, Fondmetal and Speedline. Because the rear tyres have a higher workload, the maximum permissible rear wheel rim width is employed. The team and the tyre manufacturer then jointly select a width for the front rims which will balance the rear. There is currently a trend towards wider front rims, up to 305 mm (12 in) and beyond.

An FIA regulation stipulates that the wheels must be designed to shear off completely in a major impact. The introduction of this regulation was a direct consequence of the accident which claimed the life of Ayrton Senna at Imola in 1994. In the subsequent investigation, Senna's fatal injuries were attributed not to the impact with the concrete wall bordering the racetrack, but to a suspension element attached to the right front wheel piercing his helmet visor and entering his skull just above the right eye socket. The wheel had broken free in the impact but had remained connected to the car by its steering arm and swung at the cockpit with immense force.

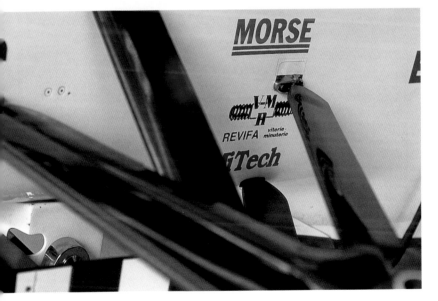

Only a few years ago, the major suspension components on Formula 1 cars – the upper and lower wishbones, and the pushrods which carry the forces to the inboard shock-absorber/spring units – were made from steel. Then some teams began to experiment by adding carbonfibre shrouds around them to improve their streamlining, and this led to the introduction of the first carbon-composite wishbones.

As the designers' confidence grew, an increasingly large proportion of the suspension was constructed in this way. A point was reached where the only metallic components in some suspension systems were a few titanium plates added as reinforcements – and now all-carbon-composite suspension systems are the norm. The weight-saving achieved by replacing a steel wishbone with a carbon-composite one is around 400 grams (14 oz), so the process has been well worthwhile.

Most of the external suspension elements have a 'knife-edge' design to minimise air resistance.

At the outer extremities of the four suspension assemblies are the uprights. An upright is typically machined from a solid block of titanium and serves as the interfacing joint connecting the wishbones and pushrod to the axle/wheel-bearing assembly and brake unit (and, in the case of a front upright, the steering arm).

The shock-absorber/spring units are mounted internally and connected to the pushrods via rocker mechanisms. At the front (pictured), they are mounted on the top of the chassis – in front of the cockpit – covered by a carbonfibre hatch; at the rear, they are mounted atop the gearbox. This is primarily to keep them out of the airflow, reducing aerodynamic drag: many years ago, they were fitted externally, between the wheels and the chassis flanks. Some cars have twin-damper systems, while others have three dampers. The shock-absorbers are supplied to the teams by proprietary manufacturers, including Sachs and Bilstein, although teams often collaborate with their suppliers on damper design.

Some suspension systems cope better than others when a car 'rides the kerbs', allowing the driver to use the kerbs to his advantage when choosing his racing line. Sometimes a car just kisses a kerb with a tyre, kicking up a telltale cloud of dust but causing no problems. But on other occasions a car can strike a kerb hard, sending a fierce shock through the suspension – or, worse, fly into the air and land heavily, which can cause major suspension damage and also damage other parts of the car.

As well as complex and powerful structural loadings, the rear suspension is subjected to thermal stresses, as it is fixed to structures which reach temperatures in excess of 120 degrees C in the vicinity of the exhaust system.

The better-equipped teams test the dynamic performance of the suspension on a static test rig in the comfort of their headquarters. The car is mounted on a complex system of hydraulics which imposes loadings duplicating those fed into the car on the racetrack. The hydraulics are commanded by software downloaded from previous runs on specific circuits and captured on the car's on-board instrumentation. The static test rig can simulate, for example, the loads which are fed into the front and rear suspension in high-speed corners, including the bumps in the racetrack surface. Braking and acceleration loadings can be fed in simultaneously – and aerodynamic loadings can also be fed in, either independently or simultaneously.

Energetic driving of the type pictured here reflects the exuberance of the Jordan team. Based just outside the main entrance to the Silverstone circuit, Jordan has all of the ingredients of success but has so far failed to find race-winning form.

FIA regulations stipulate that all four wheels must be fitted to the car five minutes prior to the start of the race. Any car with its wheels not fitted at the time of the five-minute signal must start from either the pitlane or the back of the grid. If rain starts between the five-minute signal and the start of the race, the Race Director may permit teams to change tyres. In this situation, abort lights are illuminated and the countdown to the start of the race begins again at the 15-minute point.

Once the red lights have come on, the drivers must hold their cars against the brakes and not allow them to creep forward. With the exception of the Monaco Grand Prix, sensors are embedded in the racetrack surface under every car on the starting grid, and aboard every car. This network of sensors acts as a tell-tale if any driver attempts to jump the start. It is difficult to prevent the car from creeping on the grid, but the driver must prevent this happening at all costs, because if any relative movement is recorded between the sensor in the racetrack surface and the sensor on the car, a time penalty will be incurred – entailing a trip down the length of the pitlane within three laps of the team being notified of the infringement, and a ten-second period at a complete standstill under the watchful eye of an FIA official.

The task of preventing the car from creeping is made even more difficult at circuits which have their start line on a steeply descending straight – for example, the Suzuka circuit in Japan.

When the red lights go out, the race is on. In clouds of blue tyre-smoke, the cars accelerate savagely away from their starting positions and the drivers jockey for position into the first corner – where there is often physical contact as drivers attempt to gain the most advantageous racing line.

The frantic dash into the first corner provides drivers with an opportunity to gain more places in a few seconds than they are likely to be able to gain in many laps of actual racing, and some – for example, McLaren's David Coulthard – have elevated it to an art form. But with so many drivers having the same aim, the chances of a first-corner accident are high.

chapter 7 THE COCKPIT ENVIRONMENT

ALTHOUGH not strictly a 'technology' item, the driver is a vital element in the functioning of a Formula 1 car, so it is only proper that we include him and his working environment, the cockpit.

The phenomenal performance of these cars places enormous physical strains on the driver. Before new grip-reducing regulations came into effect in 1998, lateral forces of over 3.5 G were being experienced through high-speed corners – equating to a lateral load in excess of 30 kg (65 lb) being exerted on the driver's neck muscles. Even with the introduction of the new regulations, the lateral G-forces are punishing over a race distance.

Some corners – most notably Spa's spectacular S-bend, Eau Rouge – also exert a considerable compressive force on the driver's spine, because the car has to make a rapid transition from travelling downhill to travelling uphill, imposing high vertical G-loadings.

The forces of acceleration and deceleration are no less severe. The driver's neck muscles must react to almost constant fore-and-aft forces as the car rapidly gathers speed out of corners or viciously erodes speed under braking into corners. At 2 G, the accelerative forces are reasonably manageable – aided by a cockpit head-rest – but in 1997, before the grip-reducing regulations came into force, deceleration forces under braking at high-speed circuits commonly reached 4.5–4.8 G, and occasionally peaked at close to 6 G at the point when the wheels locked.

A driver's vision can be impaired by the high G-forces encountered during hard cornering and heavy braking, as the flow of blood to the eyes is affected by such forces, deteriorating peripheral vision and distorting perspective. Severe bumps in the racetrack surface can be even more disorienting, the high vertical G-forces momentarily draining the blood from the driver's eyes. At Brazil's notoriously bumpy Interlagos circuit, some corners have to be driven virtually 'blind'.

With such massive forces bearing upon them, it is little wonder that Formula 1 drivers must maintain obsessive fitness regimes to stay competitive. Their neck muscles must be developed to counter the high lateral and longitudinal G-forces, and their arms and hands must be muscular enough not only to cope with those forces, and with the vertical G-forces imposed by bumps and undulations in the racetrack surface, but also to turn the steering wheel when the 'weight' of the car has risen under the influence of high aerodynamic downforce levels at higher speeds, making the effort of steering more strenuous: a Formula 1 car 'weighs' over a ton at 240 kph (150 mph).

The human heart normally functions at 60–80 beats per minute, but at qualifying and race speeds a driver's heart rate can soar way beyond that. During a brief respite from the pressures of a qualifying session, Ulsterman Eddie Irvine is pictured examining his lap times. During qualifying for the 1997 German Grand Prix at the super-fast Hockenheim circuit, Stewart driver Rubens Barrichello's heart rate was measured as an experiment. Going into the first corner on one lap, his heart rate was 160 beats per minute, and it peaked at 190 beats per minute during the course of that lap. Heart rates as high as 210 beats per minute have been recorded during Formula 1 qualifying sessions. Such rates could be fatal to a person not totally fit.

The driver's overall fitness and stamina must be developed enough to maintain strength and concentration throughout a race lasting as long as two hours. To make matters worse, the high temperatures experienced in certain countries – where cockpit temperatures can soar to 50 degrees C – are exacerbated by the multi-layered fireproof garments the drivers wear. Dehydration also contributes to fatigue: up to a litre of body fluid may be lost during a race – around 2 kg (4 lb). Drivers sip energy-giving drinks from a small on-board bottle to help replenish some of the lost liquid and vitamins, and most adorn their nostrils with the patented stick-on plastic devices favoured by athletes to open their air passages and thereby aid breathing.

Fire is not the hazard that it used to be in Formula 1, but the risk is still taken very seriously. The drivers' overalls are composed of four layers of a lightweight flame-resistant material. The layers – and the stitching – are a weave of Nomex fibres, a patented product from Du Pont containing Kevlar. FIA regulations stipulate that an 800-degree C liquid propane flame be blasted onto a section of fabric for 12 seconds to verify its flame-resistance. This test results in severe damage to the outer layer, but protection is such that the inner layer sustains

only moderate scorching. In actual fact, the overalls will protect the driver for 30 seconds against direct flame penetration.

As a testimony to the protective qualities of the fire-proof clothing, there was no better example than Dutch driver Jos Verstappen's spectacular refuelling accident in the Benetton pit during the 1994 German Grand Prix at Hockenheim. A more recent set of Verstappen's racewear – worn during his 1997 season with Tyrrell – is pictured here.

Under their overalls, drivers wear a long-sleeved roll-neck Nomex vest; a few wear 'long johns' for extra protection. The knees, elbows and ankles can be subjected to painful knocks within the confines of the cockpit, so many drivers fit additional padding to those areas. Their Nomex gloves have extra padding to guard their knuckles, and suede palms to protect against blistering and improve their grip on the steering wheel. For fire-protection combined with dexterity on the foot pedals, the drivers wear Nomex-lined suede boots over their fireproof socks, and under their FIA-approved crash-helmets they wear a Nomex balaclava.

FIA inspectors examine the drivers' protective garments during scrutineering, and also undertake random spot-checks after races.

For comfort – and style! – drivers' overalls are custom-made, but they are also highly functional. For example, the epaulettes are specially reinforced, so that the driver can be pulled from the cockpit if he is incapacitated in an accident.

The high lateral G-forces experienced during cornering can impose a load on the hips equivalent to 100 kg (220 lb), so drivers do what they can to make their cockpit environment more comfortable. For example, Jacques Villeneuve specifies that his overalls are made without waistband pockets, so they can't rub against him, while Gerhard Berger – who retired from Formula 1 at the end of 1997 – used to specify that his overalls had the side seams repositioned for the same reason.

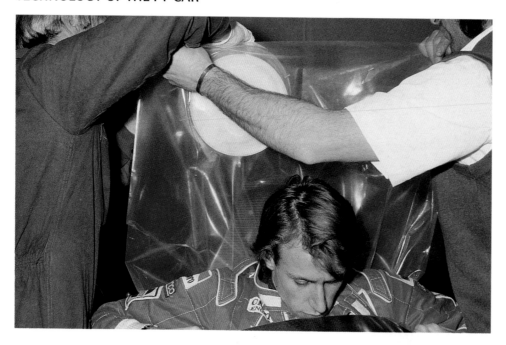

An all-important seat fitting ensures that the driver is fully supported in the car against the massive cornering, acceleration and deceleration forces he will experience, by creating a form-fitting seat profiled to his own unique body shape.

The seat-fitting takes place at the team's factory. A large plastic bag is placed in the cockpit, then the driver climbs in and sits on it. The top of the bag is held open to allow an equal mix of two chemical agents to be poured in – as pictured during this seat-fitting for Italian driver Luca Badoer. From the moment they are blended together shortly before pouring, these two agents begin a chemical reaction that creates a foam-like substance which expands within the bag and then solidifies, conforming exactly to the driver's contours.

Whilst this chemical reaction is in its final stages, the driver must maintain what he feels is a comfortable position in the car, supporting himself until the foam begins to harden, and then – at the critical point as he feels the foam solidifying – uses the bag as a seat, allowing it to support him. When the bag is removed, excess foam is trimmed from the edges, then the seat is given several coats of resin to harden it further, ensuring it will withstand the rigours of racetrack use.

The driver takes this form-fitting seat with him from one chassis to another if he switches to the spare car – as Jarno Trulli is doing after crashing his car in qualifying – or that of his team-mate.

In future, seats are likely to become a safety feature, by being rapidly removable – thereby allowing an injured driver to be lifted out of the car while still in his seat. This would significantly reduce the risk of aggravating spinal injuries.

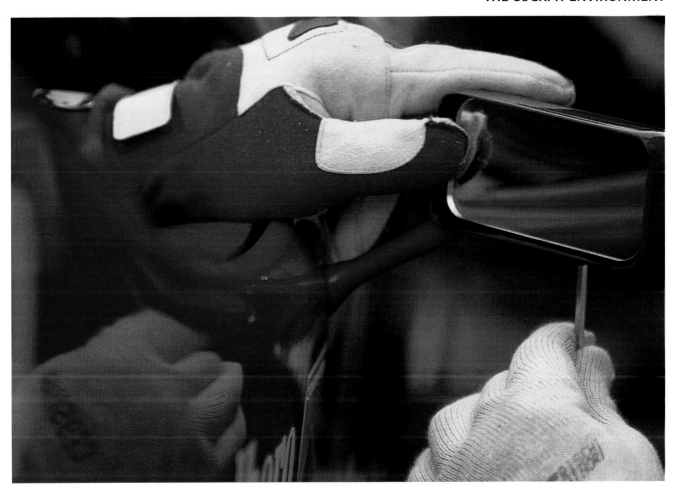

Driver vision is a vital consideration when the car is designed. The quality of the driver's view forwards is vitally important for obvious reasons, but his view backwards is also critical – from the standpoints of both racecraft and safety. Unless he has an awareness of the relative positions of his opponents' cars, he cannot adequately defend his racing line. Worse, he may pose a hazard to faster cars. The sizing and positioning of the rear-view mirrors are therefore critical, and both are governed by the regulations – being verified by FIA inspectors with a visual recognition test using numbered boards placed behind the car.

For 1998, the regulations called for a 20-mm (0.8-in) increase in the width of the rear-view mirrors to 120 mm (4.75 in). The depth of the mirrors remained the same at 50 mm (1.95 in).

While concentrating on driving his car to its full potential and taking into account the relative positions of his opponents' cars, a driver may occasionally miss a trackside flag signal – with dire consequences. Heavy fines, and even disqualification, can result if a driver fails to respond to a warning flag, either because he was preoccupied or because his view of the flag was obscured by another car. Formula 1 cockpits could in future be fitted with a system of coded lights to prevent this happening. The lights would be triggered by transponders sited at regular intervals around the racetrack. Traditional flags would still be used in parallel.

THE COCKPIT ENVIRONMENT

As well as bearing several key controls, most Formula 1 steering wheels also carry most of the instruments, including the digital rpm, oil pressure and fuel-state indicators, a row of gearshifting lights and various warning lights. Most steering wheels are constructed entirely of carbonfibre. They must be rapidly removable to provide adequate clearance for the driver to climb from the cockpit in an emergency, or be lifted out if he is incapacitated.

A mechanism at the top of the steering column is pulled back to release the wheel.

FIA regulations demand that the maximum time required for the driver to evacuate the cockpit and replace the steering wheel is ten seconds. Drivers are fined if they do not replace the steering wheel after abandoning their car, as this creates difficulties for track-side marshals attempting to manoeuvre the car quickly to a place of safety.

Although the new regulations introduced for 1998 required the cars to be ten per cent narrower, they also demanded that the cockpit must become wider, to make it quicker and easier for the driver to get out: the minimum permissible dimensions of the chassis at the point where the driver's torso is located have increased from 25 cm (9.75 in) to 30 cm (11.75 in) square.

For lightness and precision, the steering column is 'gun-barrelled' from a solid bar of steel. The trend towards high noses in Formula 1 has resulted in steering columns becoming virtually horizontal. A complex set of gears and bevels is then required to convert the driver's steering inputs through almost 90 degrees to the steering rack.

To cater for driver preferences, steering columns are adjustable. Gerhard Berger is 194 cm (6 ft 4 in) tall, so adjustments had to be made to the steering column to prevent its obstructing his knees. And with space so limited in the tight confines of the cockpit, Damon Hill's larger-than-average feet are said to present challenges!

Steering racks have evolved considerably in recent years, becoming lighter and more efficient as a result of better materials and design, and a shift away from proprietary to purpose-made racks which have much greater resistance to wear. Previously, wear in the rack and pinion during the course of a race introduced unwelcome 'play' into the steering.

Some cars have power-assisted steering. This typically offers 30 per cent assistance, which is sufficient to ease some of the physical strain of driving the car without removing all-important 'feel' from the steering system.

The gear-change activator is sited immediately behind the steering wheel and takes the form of two paddles operated by the fingertips: the left-hand paddle for downshifts, the right-hand paddle for upshifts (it is necessary for the driver to have almost full throttle before the system will accept an upshift).

It is a semi-automatic system which provides a silky-smooth transition from gear to gear and makes it virtually impossible for the driver to miss a gear, because gearchanges are accomplished in sequential order, both up and down. While the driver keeps his hands firmly on the steering wheel, electronics operate hydraulic actuators which simultaneously change the gears and operate the clutch – making gearshifts almost ten times faster (an average of 20 milliseconds) than they would be with a wholly mechanical system.

Close to hand is the brake-bias adjuster, which allows the driver to alter the comparative braking effort between the front and rear wheels to help avoid locking one pair under heavy braking.

A car can, if the driver so wishes, be fitted with an electronic handbrake. Although this can bring certain advantages, a key drawback of an electronic handbrake is the fact that the driver often finds it difficult to sense how much the clutch is 'biting' as it starts to engage – and therefore risks making a mediocre start – whereas a brake *pedal* offers better 'feel'.

Electronic handbrakes have posed other difficulties in the past – most notably when Benetton drivers Gerhard Berger and Jean Alesi were left at an ignominious standstill on the starting grid for the 1996 European Grand Prix at the Nürburgring, their electronic handbrakes stuck in the 'on' position!

TECHNOLOGY OF THE F1 CAR

Formula 1 drivers are strapped firmly into their cars with a multi-point safety harness comprising two shoulder straps, two abdominal straps and two crotch straps. The shoulder straps are heavily padded at the points where they come into contact with the driver's collar bones.

FIA regulations stipulate that the straps must be 75 mm (2.95 in) wide and be connected by a quick-release buckle which enables the driver to release the belts and climb from the car in no more than five seconds.

Safety harnesses can be tested to the limit in an accident as severe as the near-fatal one which befell Mika Häkkinen during practice for the 1995 Australian Grand Prix at Adelaide. Häkkinen's McLaren suffered a puncture, which hurtled it into the guardrail at very high speed. Such was the severity of the impact that the stretching of the safety harness and the elastication of Häkkinen's body resulted in his head striking the steering wheel, fracturing his skull and causing major brain trauma – from which he fortunately fully recovered.

Such injuries could have been prevented by having a deformable structure built into the steering wheel or a collapsible steering column. This has since become a mandatory requirement. An alternative solution would be an airbag. Following extensive research and experimentation, airbags are likely to be seen in Formula 1 cars in the not-too-distant future, provided a design can be perfected which does not endanger the driver on inflation or hinder his escape or extraction from the cockpit. If and when they do appear, they are likely to take the form of a small bag mounted in the centre of the steering wheel.

To provide additional protection for the driver's head in the event of a major accident, Formula 1 cars are fitted with a 'collar' of deformable padding which extends virtually right around the cockpit opening. Strict regulations govern the dimensions and positioning of the FIA-approved padding material, which must be 75 mm (2.95 in) thick, must extend as far forward as the steering wheel, and must be removable without the need for tools.

The introduction of these 'collars' came as a direct result of the accident which almost claimed the life of the Austrian driver Karl Wendlinger during practice for the 1994 Monaco Grand Prix. Wendlinger's Sauber struck a protective water barrel positioned in front of a guardrail at a relatively modest speed, but his exposed head received a vicious blow which ultimately ended his Grand Prix career.

In another measure designed to provide greater protection for the driver's head, the sides of Formula 1 cockpits are higher than they were a few years ago. FIA regulations stipulate that the cockpit sides must be no lower than 22 cm (8.6 in) below the imaginary line connecting the rollover hoop and the rollover reinforcement immediately in front of the cockpit aperture: the latter often takes the form of a triangular protrusion just in front of the cockpit lip. The top of the driver's helmet must be at least 5 cm (1.95 in) below this imaginary line.

To protect against the risk of fire or electrocution in the event of an accident, FIA regulations decree that the driver must be able to kill the electrical circuits to the ignition, fuel pumps and high-intensity rear light by means of a spark-proof circuit-breaker switch on the dashpanel. Its position must be marked by a master switch identification triangle. In addition, an external cut-off switch – which takes the form of a D-shaped handle located on the right side of the rollover hoop – must be operable from a safe distance by a hook in an emergency.

This handle has a dual purpose, because it also serves as the external activation switch for the car's fire-extinguisher system. Its location is denoted by a circular *E* (for 'Extinguisher') symbol. FIA regulations stipulate that the fire-extinguisher system must have an independent electrical supply, and be capable of being activated both by the driver – by means of a button on the dashpanel – and externally. Fixed to the cockpit floor in the space beneath the driver's thighs, the fire extinguisher discharges into the cockpit (for 10–40 seconds) and the engine compartment (for 30–80 seconds).

In order to create a margin of safety against foot-crushing injuries, FIA regulations stipulate that the foot pedals – which are adjustable fore and aft – must never be less than 15 cm (5.9 in) aft of the front axle centre-line. The throttle pedal is situated on the right side, and has a comparable amount of travel to that of a roadgoing car. The brake pedal is situated in the middle in a three-pedal layout, as pictured, with the clutch pedal – usually used only for the start and driving out of the pits – to the left. The brake requires a deft touch – but also huge pressure: typically 150 kg (330 lb), generating well over 1000 psi in the brake lines. Power-assisted braking is banned by the regulations.

Many drivers prefer left-foot braking, in which case there is usually a two-pedal layout – brake on the left, throttle on the right – with a hand-operated clutch activator mounted on the steering wheel. However, some prefer to have a clutch pedal in addition to the hand-clutch for use in the event of a spin.

There are usually footrests mounted at the sides of the pedals. Also, some drivers like to have shallow rims added to the sides of certain pedals to ensure that their feet won't inadvertently stray onto the wrong pedal.

Both in the pits and out on the racetrack, the driver can communicate with his team via a two-way VHF radio link. Here, Jacques Villeneuve is pictured in conversation with his race engineer, Jock Clear, while Prost team boss Alain Prost and team manager Cesare Fiorio advise their drivers, Olivier Panis and Jarno Trulli, on race strategy from the pit wall.

The driver wears earplugs fitted with tiny earphones, and he has a little microphone close to his mouth, activated by a button on the steering wheel – usually marked *R* (for 'Radio'). Because the key topic of conversation is race strategy, transmissions are scrambled to prevent eavesdropping by rival teams and the media – but the FIA can demand access to the teams' tape-recordings of transmissions if they wish to investigate allegations of infringements, such as race-rigging.

This happened after the final race of the 1997 season, following allegations of collusion between the McLaren and Williams teams during the closing stages of the European Grand Prix at Jerez, Spain. When the so-called 'Jerez-gate Tapes' were handed over by both teams, they were subsequently exonerated of any wrongdoing.

Following that episode, it was proposed that teams should offer up their scramble codes to the FIA so that its officials could in future police transmissions in 'real time'. They might be entertained by some of what they hear: Jacques Villeneuve is said to have recited nursery rhymes over the radio to relieve his boredom when holding a comfortable lead in certain Grands Prix during his World Championship-winning year of 1997!

TECHNOLOGY OF THE F1 CAR

The way in which Formula 1 drivers exercised their skills in the cockpit was something of a mystery until the emergence of telemetry. Now, all of the driver's inputs through the steering wheel, brake pedal, throttle pedal and other controls can be analysed in minute detail in the pit garage or back at the team's headquarters.

Telemetry is the process by which readings from sensors installed throughout the car are transmitted by radio waves to a receiver in the pit garage, where they are stored on computers and displayed on banks of monitors. As well as providing data on the driver's control inputs – such as the points at which he brakes and changes gear – the telemetry relays a constant stream of information on the performance of the engine, brakes and other key components: for example, the engine revs, engine oil temperature and oil pressure, fuel flow rate, individual brake temperatures and wear rates, and the movements of the suspension.

The telemetry transmissions are strictly one-way. FIA regulations prohibit the transmission of data *to* the car. Prior to this ban, teams telemetered commands from the pits to remotely alter the functioning of the engine and modify other key parameters to improve the car's performance in response to changing conditions out on the racetrack.